PEOPLE
IN THE NEWS

Elijah Wood

Titles in the People in the News series include:

PEOPLE
IN THE NEWS

Elijah Wood

by Terri Dougherty

**LUCENT
BOOKS®**

THOMSON

™

GALE

San Diego • Detroit • New York • San Francisco • Cleveland
New Haven, Conn. • Waterville, Maine • London • Munich

LIBRARY OF CONGRESS CATALOGING-IN-PUBLICATION DATA

Dougherty, Terri.
    Wood, Elijah / by Terri Dougherty
        p. cm. — (People in the News)
Summary: A biography of Elijah Wood, from his childhood in Iowa to the new opportu-
nities brought by his starring role in the film, "Lord of the Rings."
Includes bibliographical references and index.
    ISBN 1-59018-448-3 (hardback : alk. paper)
    1. Wood, Elijah 1981– —Juvenile literature. 2. Motion picture actors and actresses—
United States—Biography—Juvenile literature. [1. Wood, Elijah, 1981– 2. Actors
and actresses.] I. Title. II. People in the news (San Diego, Calif.)
PN2287.W575 D68 2004
791.43'028'092—dc21

                                                                    2003008995

Printed in the United States of America

Table of Contents

Foreword

FAME AND CELEBRITY are alluring. People are drawn to those who walk in fame's spotlight, whether they are known for great accomplishments or for notorious deeds. The lives of the famous pique public interest and attract attention, perhaps because their experiences seem in some ways so different from, yet in other ways so similar to, our own.

Newspapers, magazines, and television regularly capitalize on this fascination with celebrity by running profiles of famous people. For example, television programs such as *Entertainment Tonight* devote all of their programming to stories about entertainment and entertainers. Magazines such as *People* fill their pages with stories of the private lives of famous people. Even newspapers, newsmagazines, and television news frequently delve into the lives of well-known personalities. Despite the number of articles and programs, few provide more than a superficial glimpse at their subjects.

Lucent's People in the News series offers young readers a deeper look into the lives of today's newsmakers, the influences that have shaped them, and the impact they have had in their fields of endeavor and on other people's lives. The subjects of the series hail from many disciplines and walks of life. They include authors, musicians, athletes, political leaders, entertainers, entrepreneurs, and others who have made a mark on modern life and who, in many cases, will continue to do so for years to come.

These biographies are more than factual chronicles. Each book emphasizes the contributions, accomplishments, or deeds that have brought fame or notoriety to the individual and shows how that person has influenced modern life. Authors portray their subjects in a realistic, unsentimental light. For example, Bill Gates—the cofounder and chief executive officer of the software giant Microsoft—has been instrumental in making personal computers the most vital tool of the modern age. Few dispute his business savvy, his perseverance, or his technical expertise, yet critics say he is ruthless in his dealings with competitors and driven more by his desire to maintain Microsoft's dominance in the computer industry than by an interest in furthering technology.

In these books, young readers will encounter inspiring stories about real people who achieved success despite enormous obstacles. Oprah Winfrey—the most powerful, most watched, and wealthiest woman on television today—spent the first six years of her life in the care of her grandparents while her unwed mother sought work and a better life elsewhere. Her adolescence was colored by promiscuity, pregnancy at age fourteen, rape, and sexual abuse.

Each author documents and supports his or her work with an array of primary and secondary source quotations taken from diaries, letters, speeches, and interviews. All quotes are footnoted to show readers exactly how and where biographers derive their information and provide guidance for further research. The quotations enliven the text by giving readers eyewitness views of the life and accomplishments of each person covered in the People in the News series.

In addition, each book in the series includes photographs, annotated bibliographies, timelines, and comprehensive indexes. For both the casual reader and the student researcher, the People in the News series offers insight into the lives of today's newsmakers—people who shape the way we live, work, and play in the modern age.

Introduction

Driven to Act

From the time he was barely out of kindergarten, Elijah Wood has been awing movie audiences with an incredible ability to bring emotions to life on the screen. He has been able to connect with his fellow actors and actresses in an innocent yet meaningful way, combining the naivete of youth with a captivating wisdom. His ability has impressed film critics and captured the interest of audiences.

As an actor, Wood has incredible skill. Yet perhaps the most amazing thing about him is not his ability on-screen but his life at home. He has been able to maintain a busy schedule and successful career yet steer clear of the pitfalls of success. He stays away from drugs and the Hollywood party scene. He does not make headlines over outrageous fights with his parents or his antics with his buddies. When he indulges himself, it is likely to be with a new CD or collectible figure rather than a flashy new sports car. A self-described geek, he would rather be at home playing video games than attending a glitzy event. He respects and admires his mother, whom he credits with helping him stay grounded and keeping him from being swept up in the surreal world of moviemaking. She has helped him keep his ego in check and avoid being unduly influenced by praises and promises that often prove to be hollow.

A Grown-up Child

Success has brought with it sacrifice, however. As a child and teen, Wood never really felt like he fit in with kids his own age. His work kept him around adults most of the time, making him feel much older than he actually was. In addition, his hectic career and subsequent fame made it almost impossible for him to develop true, lasting friendships. He enjoyed his childhood and loved making movies, but his experiences and social relationships were very different from what is thought of as a typical childhood. Wood's relationship with his father also suffered as his career grew more intense. The family moved from Iowa to California to support Wood's career, but his acting jobs often took him and his mother away from home. His relationship with his father was a fragile one, and the distance his career placed between them wore it down until there was nothing left.

As a child actor, Wood was not able to experience the usual rhythms of childhood. His life has been a constant series of auditions and tryouts, successes and failures. He has been shielded from both the bland and exciting nuances that occur naturally

A young Elijah Wood (right) in a scene from the 1990 film Avalon. *As a child actor Wood had very little time to enjoy his childhood.*

Elijah Wood poses with Peter Jackson director of the Lord of the Rings, *and his wife at the 74th Academy Awards. The* Lord of the Rings *trilogy is Wood's most successful work to date.*

when life is not a constant series of acceptances and rejections. He has been fortunate to have stayed busy with his work, but there have been a few times in his life when he has had to think about what he would do if he was not busy hopping from one project to the next. When faced with those times, he has felt uncomfortable and lost.

But downtime has been rare for Wood. He has had a career that for most of his life has kept him busy as an actor yet has not overwhelmed him with fame. His volume of work provided him with the professionalism he needed for the extended *Lord of the Rings* movie shoot in New Zealand, and while there he learned things about friendship and trust that he had missed as a child. He has wisely listened to his practical mother and avoided becoming overwhelmed by the praises and material desires that trip up many talented actors. Many child actors find it difficult to make a smooth transition into an active adult career, but Elijah Wood has managed to keep working and looks forward to a long career.

Chapter 1

Opening Act

Eᴌɪᴊᴀʜ Wᴏᴏᴅ ᴡᴀs born in Cedar Rapids, Iowa, on January 28, 1981, to Deborah and Warren Wood. He spent the first six years of his life in Cedar Rapids, living with his parents, brother, and sister. All the children in Elijah's family received religious names from their parents, a reflection of his mother's Roman Catholic faith. Elijah was named after a prophet. His brother, Zachariah, who is six years older than Elijah, also had a prophet as his namesake, while his sister, Hannah, who is three years younger than Elijah, was named after the mother of the prophet Samuel.

Although he was named after a religious figure, Elijah did not spend much of his young life quietly contemplating serious subjects such as religion. He was a rambunctious youngster who did not like to sit still for long. When he was two years old, he locked his mother out of the house. As she peered in at him through a window, he happily climbed on the counters and made a mess in the kitchen. His mother eventually made her way back into the house, but it was not the last time Sparkplug, as Elijah was called by his family, tired his mother out with his energetic antics. His interest in climbing around the house also earned him the nickname "Monkey." "I used to climb on everything," Elijah later recalled. "I was always causing trouble." [1]

Model Child

In kindergarten, Elijah showed his first interest in acting when he took a chorus role in an elementary school production of *The Sound of Music*. He also played the wizard in a musical production of *The Wizard of Oz* at his school. Like many children, he enjoyed dressing up in costumes. When he was about four or five, he was dressed in a costume that he could not get out of in time to use the bathroom. He ended up having an accident, and he learned what it felt like to be extremely embarrassed.

The incident did not keep him from continuing to be an energetic handful at home, however, and his mother was not sure how to contain her son's exuberance. When she was watching television one day and saw children acting in commercials, a thought struck her. Her son seemed interested in acting, and he could likely do just as well as the other children she saw on television. She also thought acting might be a way to steer Elijah's abundant energy into more acceptable pursuits. Following her instincts, his mother enrolled six-year-old Elijah in Avant Studios, a modeling and talent school in Cedar Rapids.

Elijah and Thora Birch sit in a tree in a scene from Paradise. *Birch would later play the troubled daughter in the Academy Award winning film American Beauty.*

International Modeling and Talent Association

Elijah Wood's career got its start when he was spotted by an agent at an Interntational Modeling and Talent Association (IMTA) convention. The IMTA still produces two huge conventions each year. In January, a convention is held at a Los Angeles hotel. In July, there is a convention at a hotel in New York City. The conventions give aspiring actors, models, dancers, and singers a chance to compete and show their skills to talent agents and casting directors.

Those participating in contests are grouped by age. They show their talent in competitions such as runway, monologues, and a talent showcase. The conventions also include educational seminars about the industry.

Elijah immediately took to this new activity. He attended the modeling school and went on auditions and studio calls. He landed some work in commercials and was encouraged by his success. Through his budding modeling career, he also took his first trip to California. In January 1989 he visited Los Angeles for an International Modeling and Talent Association convention.

Standing Out

The two-day convention brought together hundreds of children and young adults who were interested in modeling and acting. All were hoping to be noticed, but Elijah's abundance of energy and looks that were both interesting and eye pleasing made him stand out. His natural charisma set him apart from the other five hundred modeling and acting hopefuls at the event. During the convention, the children had the opportunity to perform in front of the judges. When he took his turn at doing a monologue, his enthusiastic rendition of his lines spoke volumes about him. Seven-year-old Elijah clearly enjoyed performing.

Elijah caught the eye of Gary Scalzo, an agent who was a judge at the convention. When the room went silent as Elijah walked onstage for his monologue, Scalzo realized Elijah had a natural stage presence that could carry him as an actor. After the show, Scalzo approached Elijah and his mother. He asked Elijah if he had ever considered acting. The question caught Elijah by surprise. He had gone to the convention with the idea of perhaps landing modeling jobs in commercials. Becoming an actor had not been his goal. Although Scalzo's ideas for Elijah's future were different from what Elijah and his mother had been planning, he agreed to give acting a try.

The next day Elijah and his mother went to Scalzo's office, where Elijah read for him. Elijah's reading and ability to follow directions impressed Scalzo. He told them that Cedar Rapids would not be the best place for Elijah and his family if they wanted to have Elijah pursue a career for which he apparently had a gift. He urged Elijah's mother to move the Wood family to California. There, Elijah would have the opportunity to audition for roles and use his natural talent for acting.

Budding Actor

Elijah's family took Scalzo's advice to heart and quickly prepared to relocate to California. A month after the modeling and talent convention, Elijah was living in California with his mother, brother, and sister. His father joined them a little while later, when it became clear that Elijah's career would require him to live near Hollywood.

Scalzo became Elijah's talent manager, and the youngster was soon busy with auditions. It took only six weeks for Elijah to land his first role. Singer Paula Abdul needed kids to act like adults in her 1989 video "Forever Your Girl," and Elijah had just the look the video's director was seeking. Dressed like a young executive, a somber-looking Elijah breaks a pencil in the video. Acting like an adult was a fitting beginning for Elijah's acting career, as he would grow up quickly in Hollywood.

Elijah soon had more roles to add to his acting resume. Later in 1989, he captured a small part in *Back to the Future II*. The movie was the second in a series of three that had Michael J. Fox's character, Marty McFly, furiously trying to fix a series of events in order to ensure his family's happiness. In Elijah's first appearance on the big screen, he tries to get a video game to work in 1980s-style diner, and Fox steps in to show him how it is done. Playing a child living in the year 2015, he shakes his head to express disbelief that Fox has to use his hands to play the game. It was small part for Elijah, but he was unfazed as he stood next to a major star while wearing a lime green beanie, and he charmingly chided the veteran actor with his smug look.

Back to The Future

The movie *Back to the Future II* gave Elijah Wood the opportunity for a small part in a big movie. *Back to the Future II* was the second of three movies that had star Michael J. Fox traveling through time with mad scientist Christopher Lloyd. In the first movie, *Back to the Future,* Fox's Marty McFly travels with Lloyd to the 1950s, where he sees his parents as they were in high school and impresses kids with his skateboarding and guitar playing ability. The first movie was released in 1985 and has become a worldwide favorite and spawned two sequels and a cartoon series.

The initial movie was not meant to be the first of three, but a joke at the end that had Doc beckoning Marty back into a flying car to save his children became the catalyst for two more movies. The second and third movies, released in 1989 and 1990, were the first movie sequels to be filmed back-to-back. The first takes Fox forward to the year 2015, where he gets a glimpse of what will happen to him and his children in the future unless he can go back to 1955 and make some changes. The third takes Fox and Lloyd back to the Old West.

Michael J. Fox stars in a scene from Back to the Future II. *Wood made his acting debut in this film.*

Elijah had another tiny part in the 1990 crime drama *Internal Affairs,* which starred Richard Gere, but he got to show off his talents in a much larger way with an important role in the movie *Avalon.* Released late in 1990 when Elijah was nine years old, *Avalon* is loosely based on the life of director Barry Levinson. The story follows the life of a grandfather, Sam Krichinsky, played by Armin Mueller-Stahl, who came to America in 1914. Elijah has the pivotal role of Michael, Sam's grandson. In a role based partly on Levinson's own life, Elijah's character offers an innocent and unassuming viewpoint that is crucial to the film. He has an easy rapport with his on-screen father and grandfather and expresses a range of emotions, from distress, fear, and guilt to excitement and glee. The movie is long and complicated at times, but it touched viewers with its mixture of gentle humor and family strug-

Wood plays the part of Michael in Avalon. *Elijah's performance played a large part in the movie's success.*

gles. Elijah's performance played a large part in the movie's success. He had a presence that drew people into the story, with a wide-eyed attentiveness to other characters and fitting reactions to their statements and situations. He also delivered both humorous and insightful lines with perfect timing, and he charmed viewers with his sky blue eyes and bushy eyebrows.

Natural Ability

Avalon was nominated for several Academy Awards, and Elijah was applauded for his good work in the film. However, his role was not something he worked hard at perfecting. Acting came naturally for Elijah. After his introduction to modeling at the school in Cedar Rapids, Elijah never bothered with acting or modeling classes. Learning from the professionals he worked with, he used his understanding of people and his innate ability to deliver his lines with aplomb. He excelled in his role as a precocious child in *Avalon,* proving that he was more than just a cute kid with the ability to pose for the camera.

His mother recognized her son's ability and managed his career, but she did not force him to show off his talent or push acting jobs on her young son. She gave him the option to act or let it go. He chose to act. It was not a chore for him, but rather something enjoyable that engaged his eager young mind.

Family Impact

Elijah's enjoyment of acting translated into success for the youngster. His career bloomed quickly, and he was transformed from a young child who could not stop bounding around the house to one who adeptly followed the suggestions of movie directors and charmed audiences with his talent. His success brought changes, however. Although Elijah seemed to segue effortlessly into his new lifestyle, it was not quite as easy for his parents and siblings.

The family's life was dramatically altered in a short period of time when the Woods moved from the Midwest to the West Coast to support Elijah's career. The settled routine they had enjoyed in Iowa was gone, with the family's schedule revolving around Elijah's movie shoots and auditions. When Elijah went on location, his mother went with him, and his siblings often accompanied them

Cedar Rapids

Cedar Rapids is in the east-central part of the midwestern state of Iowa. The city, which had a population of more than 121,000 people in 2000, was established on the Cedar River and is surrounded by fertile farmland. The rolling hills around the city are covered with fields of corn, a crop the city pays tribute to with the name of its minor league baseball team, the Cedar Rapids Kernels.

Many of the jobs in the city revolve around agriculture and technology. The city boasts that it is large enough to provide job opportunities and small enough that its business and industry did not overshadow the beauty of the region. The area's lakes and rivers provide opportunities for swimming and fishing, and the region's winter weather gives rise to sports such as cross-country skiing and snowmobiling.

as well. Although it was interesting and exciting for everyone in the family to see new places, it was a different way of life for them.

With Elijah's success, it was clear that this unsettled lifestyle would not be changing anytime soon. The move from Iowa to California was not going to be temporary. The lives of everyone in the family were intertwined with Elijah's acting career, and his ability to act would keep them in California.

Elijah's parents, who had owned a deli in Iowa, took on new roles when the family moved to California and Elijah's career took off. His mother guided her son's career, while his father decided to look for an employer rather than launch another business. He landed a job with Federal Express, and later took a job with a company selling air cleaning machines. Once entrepreneurs sharing their own business, his mother and father were doing work that was very different from what they had been doing before Elijah's acting talent blossomed into a full-fledged career.

School Blues

Elijah's career had an impact on his duties as well. A child's main responsibility is to go to school, and it was not easy for him to attend classes and meet the demands of casting departments and movie schedules. He attended regular school for three years, but was always being pulled out of class for auditions and moviemaking. His parents decided to simplify his school life by homeschooling him, giving him the flexibility to schedule his school-work around his film career.

Elijah was more than happy to make the change. Although this meant he would lose daily contact with children his age, it would streamline his schedule so he could set aside the time he needed for both his career and school. Learning from his mother or a tutor who could be with him on location would make his life a little less fragmented, and it allowed him to combine his budding acting career with his obligations as a student.

As for the social side of the adjustment, Elijah was not heartbroken over leaving his school friends. He had spent so much time away from them while attending to the demands of his career that he did not feel a special closeness to his peers. His interests veered more toward acting than playing with his friends,

Wood watches television in a scene from Avalon. *Because Elijah was educated at home and spent most of his time on movie sets he had little interaction with kids his own age.*

and he was not especially happy when interacting with large groups of other children. When he was acting or auditioning he was mainly around adults, and he felt comfortable in their world. It was easier for him to work with grown-ups than share jokes with other kids. As he concentrated on learning lines and following a director's suggestions, he became more adept at acting than making new friends among his peers and mastering the art of playground etiquette. He did not see his lack of peer interaction as a drawback, however. He was doing something he loved and was happy with his life.

Elijah's life had gone through many changes in a few years. He discovered that he had a knack for acting, moved to a new state, and started and left a new school. Every time he auditioned for a part or acted in a movie he had to please the director or other adults in charge in a new way. But Elijah was young and flexible enough to adjust to his new lifestyle. He successfully took the untamed energy he had as a preschooler and channeled it into acting. He learned to take direction well and had no problem acting like a polite child offscreen and a little adult on-screen.

Chapter 2

Acting for Adults

Eᴌɪᴊᴀʜ's ᴇᴀʀʟʏ ᴄᴀʀᴇᴇʀ consisted mainly of serious movies that were aimed at an audience many years older than him. Rather than lighthearted television series, comedies, or movies with large casts of children, his first movies were generally made up of older cast members and were targeted at families or adults, rather than

Elijah Wood appears in a scene from the drama Radio Flyer. *The film deals with the serious topic of child abuse.*

being made for kids. *Back to the Future II* was aimed at recapturing the audience of teens and young adults who had found the first movie so appealing. While it contained little that would be objectionable for children to see, its complicated plot line, which had the movie's characters interacting with themselves and others from the first movie, was too tangled for kids Elijah's age to enjoy. *Avalon* targeted a more mature audience with its themes of coping and endurance in the face of difficult situations. Although it contained lighthearted moments, it was most appreciated by viewers who could identify with the struggles and ironic situations the family members faced through the years.

Elijah's gravitation toward movies for adults would prove to be a strong move in his fledgling acting career. His involvement in pictures with few other children helped put him in the spotlight, as he shone on-screen as a wise child rather than getting lost in a sea of cute faces. When a scene called for a young person's perspective, the focus naturally was put upon him. As a result, he did not have to fight for on-screen recognition and could play his roles with a subtle confidence that enhanced his acting ability.

Tougher Roles

As Elijah's career progressed, his roles became more challenging. He was asked to show a broader range of emotions, relying less on his innocent cuteness and more on his ability to express feel-

Thora Birch

Like Elijah Wood, Thora Birch was a child actor who would go on to have a Hollywood career after outgrowing her cherubic cuteness. Born on March 11, 1982, in Los Angeles, her baby-sitter thought she had acting potential and encouraged her parents to have her give it a try. Birch began her acting career by appearing in commercials and also appeared in television shows such as the 1988 sitcom *Day by Day*.

Birch began appearing in major movies in 1991, when she appeared in *Paradise* with Wood and in the holiday movie *All I Want for Christmas*. She also played Harrison Ford's daughter in the 1992 movie *Patriot Games* and in the 1994 movie *Clear and Present Danger*. She received a good deal of attention for her part in the 1999 Oscar winner *American Beauty*, in which she played the teenage daughter of an unhappy couple.

ings. The expressive range of emotions he had shown in *Avalon* led people to expect similar things of him in other movies. Although he enjoyed what he was doing, Elijah learned that having an acting career took hard work; acting was a business, not a playful romp. He approached his work seriously, but truly enjoyed what he was doing.

As skilled as he was for someone his age, Elijah was not always able to carry a scene with the emotion the part required. Elijah encountered one such challenging role in the television movie *Child of the Night*. The mystery, starting JoBeth Williams and Tom Skerritt, had Elijah playing an eight-year-old child who was traumatized after seeing his father killed at a Seattle marina. Williams was a psychologist helping him cope with the ordeal, and Skerritt played a detective investigating the man's death. The role called for Elijah to act out a series of Peter Pan fantasies. This was a difficult task, and Elijah's usual top-notch acting ability did not come across. But rather than place the blame on Elijah for a less than stellar performance, one reviewer questioned the depth of the task Elijah was given. "The boy is called upon to do much more than he's able to,"[2] said reviewer David Hiltbrand.

Bouncing Back

Elijah did not let a tough role deter him from acting. He still enjoyed the process of bringing lines to life, and he went on to a larger role the next year in *Paradise*. At age ten he was paired with Don Johnson and Melanie Griffith in the 1991 movie, which dealt with a family tragedy and had heart-tugging themes of grief, acceptance, and hope.

Johnson and Griffith played parents mourning the death of their son. Elijah played a ten-year-old boy from the city who came to live with them in a small town as they all faced difficult times in their lives. Elijah's turn as a troubled city boy who spends the summer in the small country town of Paradise gave him a chance to show off his skills as a dramatic actor. He is called upon to be the catalyst that helps Johnson and Griffith mend their troubled relationship, while overcoming his own fears of becoming close to others. His character also learns to trust and grows up that summer, forming a friendship with a nine-year-old girl played by Thora

Birch. The role of a precocious but misunderstood and neglected youth is one Elijah has continued to tackle many times in his acting career, and in *Paradise* he seemed to do it with ease.

In the movie *Paradise,* Elijah's character was sent to live with Johnson and Griffith because his parents' relationship was falling apart. In real life, the situation in Elijah's own family formed an eerie parallel with his character's. Although he still got along well with his mother, who accompanied him to all his movie sets, his relationship with his father was becoming distant. As his career intensified, the two of them grew more disconnected.

Dayo

There was little time for Elijah to think about his father as he quickly received an offer for another role. Elijah's next project was a 1992 *Disney Night at the Movies* presentation called *Dayo*. Starting Delta Burke, the movie showed how healthy it can be to have an imaginary friend. Elijah played the imaginary friend from Burke's childhood who helped her sort through issues involving her father, husband, and career. While the movie's premise sounds like the basis for a lighthearted comedy, the movie had some serious overtones to it. Burke's character was often melancholy and overwhelmed by the responsibility of keeping her family's business afloat. The movie had a happy ending, however, and Elijah was applauded for his impish portrayal of Burke's imaginary friend. Once again, he showed that he could take ordinary material and give it a special glow.

Although *Dayo* had some serious moments, it also had a comic touch and wrapped up with a pleasant ending for the characters. Not all of Elijah's movies would end as neatly. Actors often try to juxtapose lighter roles with more serious ones to show the depth of their ability, and Elijah was no different. His next movie, *Radio Flyer,* dealt with very serious subject matter.

A Serious Role

Radio Flyer looked at the impact of child abuse and was about a boy and his brother who fantasize about escaping from their abusive stepfather. Loraine Bracco played Elijah's mother, and Adam Baldwin had the role of the monstrous stepfather. Longing to get

Elijah Wood and Joseph Mazzello appear with a German Shepherd in Radio Flyer. *The movie's director was very impressed with Elijah.*

away from the horrible life with their stepfather, the boys contrive imaginative ways to escape. One is a fantasy flight in their red toy wagon. The movie tried to deliver a serious message about child abuse but ended up being too muddled to capture the hearts of audiences. It suffered from delays in production and a change in directors. It fell short of its goal of delivering its serious message and was universally panned.

However, Elijah's experience making the mediocre, somber movie that *Radio Flyer* became was quite different from the movie itself. Although the story was a grim one, its serious overtones did not stop Elijah from enjoying his time on the movie set. He liked the meaty role he was given and also enjoyed working with the dogs that were part of the story. With his mop of hair, innocent eyes, and ability to fall into his character, Elijah also won praise from the movie's director. "Elijah was so pure," said director Richard Donner. "He was so pure, so naïve—you look through his eyes and you see no harm, no pain, nothing but happiness."[3]

A Difficult Decision

While Elijah still enjoyed making movies, he began to see how the amount of work he was doing was taking a toll on his childhood. The ten-year-old started to wonder if he was missing something. He had been making movies and acting steadily practically since the family moved to California when he was eight, and for first time since he had agreed to give acting a try he questioned whether it was something he wanted to keep doing.

The recognition that came with being in movies was also beginning to make him uncomfortable. It bothered him that some of the mothers in his neighborhood thought he would be the perfect prop to spice up their daughters' birthday parties and did not hesitate to stop by his house and see if he would put in an appearance. Elijah adamantly refused. He did not want to be put on display. He did not want to be famous. He made movies because he enjoyed acting.

Now Elijah had to weigh the enjoyment he got from making movies against the commitment a career required. He was not certain if the emotional rewards of acting were enough to outweigh the unwanted attention he received and the parts of childhood that he was missing. Elijah's childhood had not included regular schooltime and friendships, sleepovers with his buddies, or Saturday morning soccer practice. His time was spent on movie locations, working in the world of adults and trying to please them with his acting. While missing out on typical childhood activities had never bothered him before, he now had second thoughts. Perhaps, he thought, it was time for him to set aside the pressures of a career and see what it was like to be just a kid.

However, Elijah found that being just a kid was not the easiest thing in the world, especially when he was not used to dealing with his peers. His busy movie schedule had left him with little time to forge friendships. He also did not have class assignments and after-school activities in common with others his age.

Elijah and his sister Hannah Wood pose at a movie premiere. Hannah tried acting but she had difficulty speaking her lines and conveying emotions.

Mel Gibson

Elijah Wood did well to hold his own on the screen when paired with Mel Gibson, an actor who has been of one of the most popular movie stars in America for more than twenty years. Gibson commands a top salary in Hollywood, and his good looks have earned him a spot on lists of the most beautiful people. Devoted to his family, Gibson has seven children and has been married to Robyn Moore since 1980.

Gibson, who was raised in Australia, caught the attention of moviegoers around the world with his appearance in the 1979 movie *Mad Max*. The film set the tone for his career of portraying edgy characters. He and Danny Glover starred in the 1987 movie *Lethal Weapon,* a thriller that gave way to several sequels. He also had notable turns in *Braveheart* and *The Patriot.* On the sets of his movies he is known for a love of puns and practical jokes.

Mel Gibson gives Elijah's character a flying lesson in Forever Young. *Elijah later said that Gibson was one of his favorite people to work with.*

And when he found a friend, it was difficult for him to tell whether the person liked him for the person he was or because he was mildly famous and had been in movies. Instead of chatting about music or sports, all these new friends wanted to talk about was Elijah's acting.

Elijah knew the decision was his to make. His mother managed his career, but she never forced him to act. Whether or not he continued with his acting career was Elijah's choice. His mother wanted him to pursue his career only if it was something he truly wanted to do.

After giving the matter due consideration and wrestling with his decision, Elijah decided that he enjoyed acting too much to give it up. When he was not involved in auditions and movie shoots, he missed them. He knew he would not have the same type of childhood experiences other children had and that he might miss out on some boyhood friendships, but he decided the sacrifice was worth it. Elijah's childhood was taking him down a different path than other children followed, but his alternate route was both fulfilling and fun for him. "I'm so glad I said OK," he said a few years later. "Because acting is my life now. I love it so much, meeting all the wonderful people, going on locations, playing different roles and stuff. It's really exciting."[4]

Family Ties

Although Elijah had few friends his age, he was very close to his brother and sister. They often accompanied him to movie locations and were tutored on the set as he was. Their mother was also with them, overseeing Elijah's work on location. Their father stayed home to tend to his own job, however, putting a physical distance between himself and his family that deepened their growing emotional void.

Except for his relationship with his father, Elijah considered his tight family ties an adequate substitute for close friendships. The friendship he had with his brother and sister gave him the support he needed from people close to his age. Their relationship was not perfect, however. Like all siblings they had their differences, and their childhood squabbles were sometimes enhanced by the attention Elijah received because of his acting career.

Both Zachary and Hannah had given acting a try, but had not fallen in love with it the way Elijah had. Zachary appeared in a few commercials before decided acting was not for him, and Hannah found that she was too shy to convey her emotions in front of an audience in a way that came so naturally to Elijah. She got the giggles whenever she tried to say her lines and soon realized that acting was best left to her brother.

At times Hannah resented the attention her brother's career brought him. With time, however, her feelings softened, and she became her brother's friend. She happily accompanied him to movie premieres, occasionally sharing the special event with a friend. Elijah was close to his brother as well. Although they were six years apart in age, the brothers developed a common interest in watching sports and playing video games.

Forever Young

Elijah's hesitation over his career passed quickly, and his acting jobs were soon taking him and his family, minus his father, all over the country. In his next movie, *Forever Young,* Elijah got to work in Maine with actor Mel Gibson and later called Gibson one of his favorite people to work with. Gibson had a reputation for playing practical jokes on people on the set, and his easygoing style and sense of humor clicked with Elijah.

Made in mid-1992 and released later that year, *Forever Young* follows a brokenhearted aviator who is frozen in a military experiment in the late 1930s and woken up more than fifty years later by Elijah. Elijah plays a brightly mischievous but kind youth who wakes Gibson up by accident while playing with the knobs on the unit that had kept him frozen. In the movie, Elijah has the chance to express a range of emotions, from fear to sadness to joy, and is able to make them all come across believably. He even has the chance to sing, crooning "You Are My Sunshine" to a young girl his character has a crush on. The scene is made humorous by the seriousness Elijah gives to his rendition of the song.

While Jamie Lee Curtis plays Elijah's mother and has a romantic moment with Gibson, it is the relationship between Elijah and Gibson that gives the movie its heart. Their bond is evident in a scene set in a tree house, in which aviator Gibson gives Elijah a flying lesson. Of the main characters in the movie, Elijah seemed to be most comfortable with the role he played. The other actors struggled at times, but Elijah smoothly pulled off his role of an insightful child. "The only performer who isn't miscast is Wood, who's delightful—he's smart without being a smarty-pants,"[5] wrote reviewer Ty Burr.

Huckleberry Finn

A new challenge awaited Elijah on the set of his next picture. Up to this point, he had been cast in supporting roles. Although the characters he played were integral to the story being told, the main focus of the story was elsewhere. In *The Adventures of Huckleberry Finn,* he would play the title role and have more responsibility for the success or failure of the film.

The 1993 remake of the Mark Twain classic also starred Courtney B. Vance as Jim. The movie told the story of Huck's adventurous trip down the Mississippi as he ran away from his abusive father and

Huck Finn

Elijah Wood had an opportunity to play a character who delivers a powerful message in Mark Twain's *The Adventures of Huckleberry Finn*. On the surface, the story is about a boy's adventures as he travels down the Mississippi River, but it also contains some deeper messages. The story mixes excitement with comedy and some powerful commentary about society.

Huck fakes his own death to escape an abusive father and leaves with his companion, a runaway slave named Jim. Huck and Jim are both looking for freedom, and along the way Huck is forced to examine his own views of society. Jim's back is scarred from the abuse he received at the hands of his owner, convincing Huck that slavery is wrong, in spite of what he has been taught. One of the most important lessons that the story delivers is that of brotherhood, as Huck and Jim become loyal friends. Rather than play Huck as a cute, fun-loving kid, Elijah had to show how his character quietly changes and learns from his experiences.

helped Jim find freedom. Although *Huckleberry Finn* is typically thought of as a children's movie, it touches on slavery, racism, revenge, and hypocrisy. Elijah had to show how Huck changed as his eyes were opened to different layers of society. The role called for him to capture Huck's range of emotions, from the charm he used to fool others to the fear he felt when confronted by his father.

Elijah received both praise and criticism for his portrayal of Huck. Some thought he handled the complex character adeptly, while others thought he was too young and cute to portray the mischievous Huck. Although reviewer Henry Sheehan lamented that Elijah's Huck was more scamp than scoundrel, he did admire the depth of his acting ability. "From the moment we first see him besting another boy in a riverside fight, only to deflate from boastfulness to fear when he hears his pap is back in town, Wood's Huck jumps surefootedly from one emotional extreme to another,"[6] Sheehan said.

The movie was filmed in rural Mississsppi in late 1992, and Elijah enjoyed bringing Huck's adventures to life. On the set, Vance playfully gave Elijah the nickname "Jah Jah," and the pair filmed some heartfelt scenes together with Huck and Jim on the raft, floating away from one dangerous escapade and onto the next. Vance admired the relationship Elijah had with his mother, noting that she was loving and assertive about Elijah's right to be treated like a kid but not overly protective. "People had a tendency to treat Jah Jah as an adult because he was always so professional," Vance said. "But [his mother] Deborah was there for Elijah, keeping him balanced and making sure no one forgot he was an 11-year-old."[7]

Growing Up on the Set

With his success and the attention he was receiving for acting, it would have been easy for Elijah to get caught up in the world of Hollywood. But his mother tried to keep him grounded. She listened to his concerns and expected him to be well behaved. She set guidelines and counted on him to follow them, because she cared for him and did not want him to lose sight of what was truly important in his life.

Elijah and Courtney B. Vance share a laugh in The Adventures of Huckleberry Fin. Elijah won critical acclaim for his portrayal of Huck.

Elijah had a good reputation as an actor and a hard worker who was unassuming and easy to get along with on the set. Despite his success and the accolades he received from moviegoers and reviewers, Elijah was not egotistical about his work. His mother's guidance and constant, reassuring presence on the sets of his movies kept him from getting too caught up in his own fame.

Elijah had an easygoing style that helped him get along well with the child actors he worked with on movie sets, although he did not establish firm friendships with them. Although concern about a lack of close friends had at one time made Elijah waver in his commitment to his career, he realized that he was comfortable with his acting lifestyle and no longer pined for a more traditional childhood or a large group of friends his age. For Elijah, being a young actor was what childhood was all about. It was not a life that would be normal for most children, but he chose to have a different childhood. "I grew up fast mentally and didn't relate to people my own age," he said. "They were focused on the next night's homework. I was concentrating on my lifelong career."[8]

Chapter 3

Rising Star

Eᴌɪᴊᴀʜ's ꜰᴏᴄᴜꜱ ᴏɴ his career was paying off with successful movies and admiration for his talent. He was ready to grow as an actor and take on more difficult and varied roles. He enjoyed trying different parts, and he did not let a challenging role get him down. He was ready to see what else Hollywood had to offer.

Elijah's career was gradually shifting into a different mode. Most of his early movies, with the notable exception of *Huckleberry Finn,* had been primarily aimed at adult audiences. However, he was outgrowing the precocious cuteness of a child and preteen. As he grew up, he would have to find a new way to showcase his talent if he wanted to stay busy.

The key to Elijah's continued success would be for him to keep finding interesting roles that both piqued the interest of audiences and challenged him as an actor. He did not want to be so choosy that he was left without any work, but he also wanted to take on roles that he liked. He found the right combination by interspersing movies for children and families with films that were made on a more adult level. This showed his versatility as an actor and his ability to jump from one audience to another. Through it all he was growing up and attracting a sizeable female fan base. As he matured, Elijah would have to learn to deal with a new role in public, that of teen idol.

The Good Son

Soon after filming ended on the set of *Huckleberry Finn,* Elijah was on to his next project. In *The Good Son,* the twelve-year-old was presented with a role that paired him with the most popular child star of the day, Macauley Culkin. While Elijah was considered to

Elijah Wood displays his trademark charm in this scene from North.

be a very good actor and had earned many accolades for his performances, he typically was not a headliner who brought people into the theater with his name at the top of a marquee. He had worked steadily since getting into acting, but his popularity was modest. Culkin, however, the star of the humorous *Home Alone* movies, was a child superstar. Pairing Elijah and Culkin in the 1993 movie *The Good Son* seemed like a great idea. Both were known for giving solid performances, and the movie was expected to be a showcase for their abilities.

Although the movie starred the child actors, *The Good Son* was not a movie for kids. While this was typical of the films Elijah made, it was a departure from Culkin's usual fare. Culkin had made a career out of playing a smart kid who humorously one-upped the adults around him. The serious, and terrifying, themes of *The Good Son* were vastly different from those of the movies audiences were used to seeing from him.

The Good Son is a horror film that looks at the evil lurking inside a seemingly innocent child. Culkin played the boy who

Macaulay Culkin

Macaulay Culkin, Elijah Wood's costar in *The Good Son,* was the definitive child star of the late 1980s and early 1990s. Beginning with his first successful starring role in *Uncle Buck* with comedian John Candy in 1989, Culkin appeared in a series of comedies that wowed audiences. In 1990 he made the hit *Home Alone,* in which his family forgets to take him along on a vacation. In the movie he does a memorable wide-eyed, cheek-slapping gesture.

The young Culkin was a prolific moviemaker, and his films include *My Girl* (1991), *Home Alone 2: Lost in New York* (1992), *Richie Rich* (1994), and *Getting Even with Dad* (1994). His relationship with his family soured as his fame grew, however. His father, Kit, managed his career, and became disliked in the movie industry for his determination to get things done his way. A bitter split with his father caused Culkin to leave acting for six years. He returned to acting in 2000 at age twenty in a play on the London stage.

Elijah Wood and Macaulay Culkin costar in The Good Son. *Elijah received critical praise for his role in the film.*

seemed to be nice, but who in reality was manipulative and evil to the point of having a fascination with death and killing. Elijah played his opposite, a pensive and well-meaning boy searching for answers, but who was mistakenly labeled by adults as a bad child. Elijah's character was an orphan who went to live with his aunt, uncle, and cousin, played by Culkin. In the thriller, Culkin devises a sinister plot to kill his mother.

The movie's plotline is chilling, and Elijah admitted that the movie was scary to make. However, he did enjoy working with Culkin, even though the youngster had developed a reputation as a demanding actor. Elijah said the two got along great. "He likes all the kind of stuff that I like," Elijah explained. "So he was easy to get along with."[9] There was, however, some competition between the pair. In a scene in which the boys had to run together, Culkin kept whispering to Elijah that he should not pass him.

Elijah's role in the movie was supposed to be rather bland, while Culkin's evil character was designed to show the depth of this acting ability. However, many critics pointed to Elijah's portrayal of Culkin's opposite as the highlight of the movie. Actors often adore playing evil characters, as it gives them the freedom to display a deep range of emotions. Making a good character interesting is not an easy thing to do, but Elijah pulled it off. Culkin, on the other hand, stumbled in his role. "His attempt to broaden his range with the not-for-kids thriller *The Good Son*—in a part that calls for complex emotions rather than amusing reactions—comes up way short," said reviewer Glenn Kenny. "Moreover, [*The Good*] *Son* pairs Culkin with Elijah Wood, whose moving performance as the evil Culkin's opposite number pretty much steals the movie."[10] Joseph Ruben, who directed Elijah in *The Good Son,* praised him for being able to pick up subtle changes in his lines amazingly fast, even quicker than his costar Culkin. "He's just really quick," Ruben said. "Elijah can give you the same reading or different readings with a lot of facility."[11]

Although he regularly received compliments for his work, Elijah did not aspire to be as popular as his *Good Son* costar Culkin. He saw how fame sapped Culkin's privacy and sometimes made him uncomfortable. He knew life could be difficult for a child actor and was thankful he had a mother who gave him a strong sense of who he was apart from his acting career. "I'm in the business to have fun and do movies and stuff like that," he said. "Not to be famous or be a star. That's not what the business is about, not for me it isn't."[12]

Staying Busy

At age twelve, Elijah had nine major movies on his resume. He moved quickly from one project to the next, and the little downtime he had was filled with promotional appearances for the movies he had made. He conducted interviews with newspaper reporters and appeared on television talk shows such as *Good Morning America.* When he was younger, he would get nervous during interviews and have a difficult time thinking of answers to the reporters' questions. But now he was a veteran interviewee as well as a seasoned actor, and he had no problem talking about the movies he made and what he liked to do when he was not making movies.

When Elijah was home, he liked playing with the family's bearded collies, Rascal and Levi, going in-line skating, or just hanging out with his brother and sister. He was a fan of *Star Wars* director George Lucas and collected *Star Wars* characters and other action figures. He also enjoyed playing video games and hunkering down with a good book. His budding CD collection included discs by the Smashing Pumpkins. A day when he was not

The Smashing Pumpkins

Elijah Wood's favorite band, the Smashing Pumpkins, was created in 1988 by Billy Corgan, James Iha, and D'arcy Wretzky. Drummer Jimmy Chamberlain was soon added. The band became popular for its alternative brand of music. The group's first album, *Gish,* was released in 1991, and its next, *Siamese Dream,* came out in 1993. The group's release that had the most commercial success was *Mellon Collie and the Infinite Sadness,* a double album of diverse music.

The group had a dedicated fan base who appreciated the music they were able to make in spite of struggling through some difficult times. Iha and Wretzky dated and then broke up, Corgan suffered from writer's block, and Chamberlain had troubles with drugs and alcohol. When they made music together, however, their personal problems did not seem to matter. They headlined the *Lollapalooza* tour in 1996 and were welcomed by college crowds. Over the years other musicians drifted in and out of the band, but Corgan and Iha remained with the group until the Smashing Pumpkins played its final concert in 2000.

on a movie set typically revolved around taking care of his pets, doing schoolwork, exercising, and playing on his computer.

But even when he had some time off from moviemaking, he managed to fill some of it with other acting jobs. When Elijah had a little time off after making *Huckleberry Finn* and *The Good Son* and was not busy with promotional interviews, he found time to squeeze in an appearance on the television show *Homicide: Life on the Street* and be the voice of a caller on an episode of *Frasier*. And when Macauley Culkin canceled an appearance as an Oscar presenter, Elijah was asked to fill in. Elijah attributed his ability to keep going to having an abundance of energy. "Even when I'm tired, I always have that energy," he said. "I don't know what it is. I'm always happy, excited, and I always have fun. I guess I keep my energy up by just being me."[13]

North

Soon it was time for Elijah to make his next movie, the star-filled *North,* which went into production in late 1993. With *North,* Elijah got his chance to appear in a family-oriented comedy. However, his part as a troubled youngster searching for answers was not too different from many of his previous roles. He again played a child acting like an adult. The difference in this movie was that the people acting around him were either doing things that were odd, offbeat, or annoying.

The comedy, which was released summer 1994, was not full of pratfalls or physical humor, but rather placed Elijah in situations that were humorous because of their quirkiness. His character, North, is a precocious sixth-grader who is neat, athletic, and well behaved. He is also a good actor, and in a play within the movie Elijah is called upon to play Tevye in the theater classic *Fiddler on the Roof.* His character gets rave reviews for his performance and excels at everything he does. He is such a good kid, in fact, that he feels his self-centered parents are unworthy of him.

North's parents, played by Julia Louis-Dreyfus and Jason Alexander from the successful television show *Seinfeld,* ignore their perfect son. So, egged on by a lawyer played by Jon Lovitz, North goes to court to divorce his parents so he can find a mother and father who deserve a perfect child like him. Because North's search

Elijah appears as North with country music star Reba McEntire and veteran comedian Dan Aykroyd.

for a new set of parents takes him all over the United States, Elijah's character becomes the glue that holds the movie together. He is the element of consistency in a movie that jumps from one quirky set of potential parents to the next. North receives advice from veteran actor Bruce Willis at each new location, and in the movie Elijah had to interact with a large, star-studded cast that included Alan Arkin, Kathy Bates, and Dan Aykroyd.

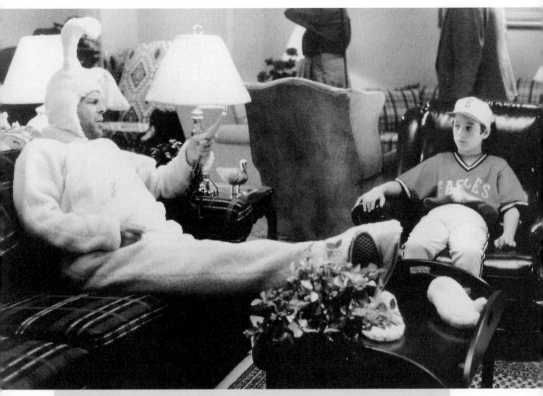

Bruce Willis appears dressed as the Easter bunny in North. *The family oriented comedy places Elijah's character in very quirky situations.*

While North remained consistently likable throughout the movie, the film's depiction of various regions of the country degenerated into stereotypes, showing Eskimos who send their grandparents out to sea on ice floes and Texans who demand the biggest and best of everything. The movie fell flat, but Elijah's costars admired his acting ability. "He's like a little man inside of a boy's body," said actress Faith Ford. "One minute he can be playing and the next minute he's just as believable as anything." [14]

The War

Elijah also rose above the material he was given in *The War,* which was released in November 1994. He played Stu, the son of a Vietnam veteran in Mississippi. His father, played by Kevin

Costner, is suffering from post-traumatic stress syndrome and cannot get a good job. Stu's life is full of pathos and troubles. He and costar Lexi Randall, who plays his sister in the movie, must protect their tree house from neighborhood bullies. The movie attempted to deliver a strong message about having something to fight for, but it failed to connect with audiences. Its parallel to the Vietnam War rang hollow, and the movie poorly portrayed Southerners.

However, Elijah's delivery of his lines and his reaction to other characters was admirable. His ability as an actor was lauded by those he worked with. "He's the first child actor I've worked with that I think is really an actor," said Jon Avnet, who directed Elijah in *The War*. "He's not tied to his cuteness." [15] Elijah's acting was called the best thing about the melodramatic movie.

Getting Noticed

Elijah was never too concerned with how his movies did at the box office or with the reviews he got. He realized that the quality of the finished product was out of his control. He did his job the best he could, enjoyed what he did, and moved on to his next project.

The quality of his performances was not going unnoticed by others, however. Elijah's talent earned him the 1994 ShoWest Award for Young Star of the Year and the Saturn Award for best juvenile performance. The thirteen-year-old appeared on television talk shows such as *Late Night with David Letterman, Regis and Kathie Lee* and *The Tonight Show with Jay Leno*. Some movie critics were hailing him as the next Culkin, a label he detested. He did not want to be compared to another child actor. He wanted the freedom to be his energetic self.

Just as she had throughout his career, Elijah's mother continued to prevent him from getting too caught up in his fame. She gave her son guidance, listened to his concerns, and made sure he did not become too self-indulgent. One way she kept his ego in check was by limiting his allowance. Although he was making a hefty salary, his allowance was a conservative ten dollars per week. He was not allowed to spend freely, usually buying Star

*Dressed in a tuxedo, Elijah Wood arrives at the 1994 Academy Awards.
That year Elijah won awards from two different organizations for his
performances.*

Wars figures or CDs when he shopped. Keeping him from irresponsibly spending the money he was earning was one way his mother made sure he stayed focused on acting for pleasure, not for money.

Elijah's family continued to be his rock, an island of stability in a world where it could be difficult for him to discern between true friends and those who only wanted to be his buddy because of his fame. He still dealt with that side of his fame by pulling away from kids his age. With his background as a child actor in adult movies, he was almost better suited for an appearance at the Oscars than dropping by the neighborhood ballpark or soccer field. It was difficult for him to trust other kids, and he was concerned that kids would not like him because of jealousy toward his status as an actor or they would only be nice to him because of his acting career. "If I were out there with kids my own age, I fear that they wouldn't like me, not because of who I am but because I'm an actor," he said. "It's scary—it's like you can't trust anybody." [16]

Just as the life of a child actor is foreign to most children, a routine of school, home, and after-school activities was foreign to Elijah. He did not want to be part of a clique or try to figure where he fit in among his peers. He knew his way around a movie set and felt comfortable in that world. He was so used to having another project on the horizon that it seemed he never sat still. "I'm kind of a monkey," he says. "I like to jump around. I can't sit down. I have to keep moving. I like moving and running around and having fun." [17]

Entering No-Man's-Land

As much as Elijah liked to work, his ability to find jobs would be tested as he entered a phase of his life that is typically a difficult time for child actors. He was a teenager now, an age that is sort of a no-man's-land for child actors. No longer a cute child, not yet an adult, it is often difficult for teen actors to find projects that suit their skills and maturity level. Even an accomplished actor like Elijah can experience a bit of a slump. After finishing *The War* in 1994, he had no movies released for more than a year. The only work he was featured in during 1995 was a Cranberries video for the song "Ridiculous Thoughts," a move that reflected his growing passion for music.

Although he was having a tough time finding the right movie for his next project, Elijah did not rush into anything. He did not feel compelled to make a rash decision, and when he was offered the role of Sandy in a movie called *Flipper* he did not say yes right away. He even asked the opinion of on-line fans in an AOL chat room. Ultimately he decided that making a movie about a dolphin would probably be fun because he would get to swim with the intelligent animals, and he traveled to Nassau in the Bahamas to costar with a dolphin.

Dolphin Delight

The role of Sandy, a city boy who goes to live with his uncle on an unnamed tropical island, proved to be a challenge for Elijah because of the character's stuck-up attitude. At the beginning of the movie, the snobbishly hip Sandy is bored and discontent, as well as oblivious to his beautiful surroundings. The only thing on his mind is leaving his uncle and catching a Red Hot Chili Peppers concert on the mainland. Elijah disliked this attitude so much that he almost turned down the role. He did not want to give anyone the impression that he condoned that type of behavior. "If the character had an attitude throughout the movie, I wouldn't have done it," said Elijah. "Whether I like it or not, I'm a role model and I take that responsibility seriously." [18]

Sandy's attitude changes as the movie progresses, and as he matures he learns to care about others through his relationship with the lovable dolphin Flipper. The movie, which updated the 1960s television series, cast Paul Hogan of *Crocodile Dundee* fame as Porter Ricks, the uncle of Elijah's character. There are also some bad guys, an adventure, and a girlfriend for Elijah thrown in for good measure.

Several dolphins shared the role of Flipper, and Elijah found working with them to be as much fun as he thought it would be. Each dolphin had its own personality, and Elijah especially liked the dolphin named Jake, which loved being around people and could make spectacular leaps out of the water. One exciting moment came when Jake did a "push-up" with Elijah, trusting him enough to push him quickly through the water like Elijah was water skiing.

It took work for Elijah to reach that level of confidence with the animals, however. He had to receive training to learn how to

Flipper

The movie *Flipper* was based on the 1960s television series, in which Luke Halpin played Sandy Ricks, the role Elijah Wood portrayed in the 1996 big screen version. In the television series, Brian Keith played Sandy's grumpy Uncle Porter Ricks, who was a marine reserve ranger. Sandy had a younger brother, Bud, played by Tommy Norden. The boys often got into trouble, or discovered that someone was planning to do something to harm their beautiful surroundings in Coral Key Park, and the day had to be saved by their pet dolphin, Flipper. One of the highlights of the series was its theme song, which sang the virtues of "Flipper, Flipper, faster than lightning." The series ran from 1964 to 1968, and was itself based on a 1963 movie, also called *Flipper*.

Elijah Wood poses with one of the dolphins that played Flipper. Elijah received special training to interact with the dolphins.

work with, feed, and care for the dolphins. It was important that the dolphins learn to trust him, so they would look to him instead of their trainers during filming. "They're so outgoing and so trusting that it was easy to make friends with them," Elijah noted, "but getting them to do things on cue is another thing."[19] One of the challenges faced by the crew was waiting for the dolphins to decide they were ready to perform. Another was the heat. On some days the temperature at the tropical location reached ninety-five degrees.

In spite of these difficulties, Elijah adored swimming, acting, and playing with the dolphins. He was surprised how difficult it was for him to leave them after filming ended. He hoped to visit the dolphins, especially Jake. "It would be really sad for me to visit and he doesn't remember me. I hope that doesn't happen,"[20] he said.

Elijah's enjoyment of working with his animal costars clearly came across on-screen, but it was also evident that he did not like his character's initial cool, cavalier attitude toward his surroundings and his uncle. Elijah tried to pull off lines such as "Gotta jet, here comes the hippie,"[21] but his delivery came across as unnatural, underscoring the fact that he and his character had little in common. Although his character was supposed to be crazy for the Red Hot Chili Peppers, in the movie Elijah wore T-shirts heralding his favorite band, the Smashing Pumpkins. The lack of common ties between himself and Sandy made it difficult for Elijah to give a consistently convincing voice to his character.

However, when his character began to shed his big-city pretensions, Elijah's portrayal improved. He shined in the movie's tender moments and ably showed his character's kind and caring side. He pulled off scenes that required him to do physical comedy, including a scene in which he groggily wakes up and steps in a bucket of water and another in which he is flipped into the ocean by a dolphin. In addition, he showed convincing fear in a scene involving a hammerhead shark.

Teen Idol

Although Elijah loved the scenes he filmed with the dolphins, there was one part of the movie that he was happy ended up on the cutting room floor. The script called for him to have a budding romance with the daughter of a marine biologist on the island. It was the first on-screen romance for Elijah, and both he and his female costar, Jessica Wesson, seemed uncomfortable with this aspect of the movie. When the script called for them to spring

Elijah apperars in a scene from The War. *As Wood matured, he began to attract the attention of female fans.*

into action alongside Flipper they were at their best, but when they were supposed to make a romantic connection the result fizzled. Elijah did not feel ready for romance in the movies or real life, and it was acutely embarrassing for him to have to show romantic feelings in front of the crew filming the movie. During

Elijah Wood narrates a story during an 1994 extravaganza produced by Disney. Elijah's strong work ethic helped him make a smooth transition from being a child actor to becoming a younger adult star.

interviews after the movie was released he winced at the memory of filming a kiss for the film. He was relieved that the scene ended up getting cut. "That was the most embarrassing thing I've ever had to do,"[22] he said.

Whether Elijah liked it or not, however, girls were noticing him, and not because it was scripted in a movie. His role as a cool, handsome teen in *Flipper* seemed made for a teen idol. Girls fell for his blue-eyed gaze, gap-toothed grin, and short, curly hair. He was moving away from the round-faced cuteness of his younger days and was developing a maturity that caught girls' eyes. The Internet was just coming into its own as a communication tool, and teens were entering chat rooms to talk about Elijah.

Although girls were clearly interested in him, Elijah was way too busy to juggle dates and his career. He insisted he was not old enough for a girlfriend, although in a magazine interview he mentioned that he admired Claire Danes of the television show *My So-Called Life*. However, consistent with his focus on his career rather than his social life, he expressed an interest in working with her rather than having a social relationship.

Career Path

Becoming a teen idol was definitely not a priority for Elijah. He was already thinking about where his movie career might take him, and he was so intently focused on that aspect of his life that he did not think about the social side. Elijah hinted that he might one day follow in the footsteps of fellow child actor Ron Howard and become a director. He also admired George Lucas, the writer and director of the *Star Wars* saga. He thought he might want to study English and improve his writing, so he could create a story with his own set of characters who followed his rules. Creating his own world was appealing to Elijah, who had for most of his life had been following someone else's script.

Since the age of six, Elijah had worked consistently in Hollywood. He was not yet a household name, but had a reputation as a solid young actor. He did not make headlines for arguments with his parents or offscreen antics with his buddies.

Instead, he made news for his blue eyes, charming looks, and wholesome attitude.

Elijah's solid performances and dependable attitude were helping him make a successful transition from child actor to young adult star. As he entered his later teen years, he had to decide if he could continue to hold on to his high moral standards when it came to the movies he chose. It would not be easy for him to find movies that had a message he agreed with, brought people into theaters, and let him grow as an actor.

Chapter 4

Experimental Phase

Eᴌɪᴊᴀʜ ꜰᴀᴄᴇᴅ ᴅɪꜰꜰɪᴄᴜʟᴛ times both on-screen and off as he entered the later part of his teen years. His career continued to move along, but at a much slower pace than it had when he was younger. The wonderful roles that had come his way almost effortlessly when he was a child were much harder to come by now that he was an older teen.

Elijah disliked parts that pigeonholed him as a typical teen, yet he could not escape the fact that he was neither right for roles as an adult or child. The most interesting roles were edgier and less wholesome than what he had been offered in the past, and he had to decide how to balance his desire to be a good role model with his wish to further his ability as an actor.

Mom Takes Charge

While he was wrestling with these career dilemmas, there were changes at home that made that side of his life difficult as well. His parents divorced in 1996, and his mother took on full responsibility for holding things together at home and dealing with Elijah's career. Her strength in the difficult situation won Elijah's admiration. "I have to thank my mom for everything in my life," he said a few years later. "She sort of overcompensated to raise the family." [23]

Elijah had been becoming emotionally distanced from his father for years. Their relationship was not bad, he later explained, it was nonexistent. "He was always physically there as a father, but never emotionally there," Elijah said. "I was not raised by my dad." [24] He tried not to let the breakup of his parents' marriage effect him. He approached it in a detached, unemotional manner,

Elijah plays the role of Mike Carver in The Ice Storm. Elijah began to take edgier roles in order to avoid becoming a typecast actor.

looking at it as the inevitable ending to a family relationship that had been growing colder and colder as the years went on. But there was a danger that he was burying feelings that could eat away at him later in life.

At home, he immersed himself in classic literature, such as *The Hunchback of Notre Dame* and *The Hobbit*. He took fencing lessons, added to his collection of *Star Wars* figures, and went in-line skating. He listened to music and bought CDs, trying to live his life as normally as possible. His Iowa-native mother knew what life was like outside the fishbowl of Hollywood and the often cutthroat business of child acting. As Elijah got older, she felt it was very important for him to realize that the praise he received for making movies and the attention he got on movie sets was not normal for a teen. "She provided a family life, completely separate from the false reality of the film industry,"[25] Elijah said.

The Ice Storm

His mother still offered guidance, but it was becoming more of Elijah's responsibility to decide where he took his career. He wanted to find roles that allowed him to showcase his acting talents yet were appropriate for a teen. He decided to shy away from lighter teen fare and opted for a dramatic role in *The Ice Storm*, a movie that features parents who focus more on satisfying their own desires than caring for their families. The children

Passion for Music

Music is one of Elijah's favorite hobbies, and over the years his tastes have run from the Beatles and Led Zeppelin to Coldplay and the Hives. The Smashing Pumpkins has been a longtime favorite, and although he has an extensive collection of their music, he still searches through the racks at the Amoeba record store in Los Angeles to see if there is something he may have missed. His CD collection runs into the thousands.

He brings part of his CD collection with him when he travels and does not hesitate to share his musical tastes with his costars. While filming *The Lord of the Rings,* he and the other actors who played hobbits would listen to music from his collection while they spent hours in the makeup trailer each morning. When he made *Try Seventeen* with actress Franka Potente and pop star Mandy Moore, he brought more than two hundred CDs to the set. He introduced Potente to the music of the Strokes and Sigur Ros, and he gave Moore an appreciation for different kinds of music. "I've kind of schooled her a bit," he said in a mtv.com news story by Ryan J. Downey. "She's recommended stuff to me as well. She has good taste—it's just different. And I don't really pretend to like the pop music. But that's cool. I certainly respect what she does." Moore agreed that Elijah's taste in music was quite different from her own. "All of the music he's really fond of and a big fan of is mostly stuff I've never heard of," she said. "The only thing that we kind of have in common are the Strokes and like Bjork and stuff, but other than that everything is over my head."

in the film act more mature than the adults, and the parents' selfish actions have fatal consequences. The movie uses a beautiful but deadly ice storm to symbolize the glittery temptations that enter people's lives, looking beautiful but ending up being heavy and destructive. Elijah credited the quality and success of the movie with allowing him to be perceived as more of an adult actor.

Christina Ricci

The Ice Storm was a breakthrough role for Elijah Wood's costar Christina Ricci as well as Wood. Both had been child actors who were beginning to take on more adult parts. *The Ice Storm* allowed them to portray young people whose innocence had faded.

Born on February 12, 1980, in Santa Monica, California, Ricci's family moved to New Jersey when she was seven. She began acting after a film critic, whose son went to school with her, was impressed with her performance in an elementary school production of *The Twelve Days of Christmas*. Her parents hired an agent for her, and Ricci began doing commercials around age eight.

Her first big role came the following year, when she played Cher's daughter in the movie *Mermaids*. She became well-known at age eleven after her likable yet morbid performance as Wednesday in the 1991 movie *The Addams Family*. She also had roles in the 1995 movie *Casper* and the 1997 remake of *That Darn Cat*, but she looked forward to playing more adult parts. In 1998 she got her wish in movies such as *The Opposite of Sex*. She has been praised for her giving a genuine quality to her performances, and like Wood is looking forward to continuing her dramatic acting career.

Christina Ricci began her acting career in 1990 at the age of ten. She has appeared in over thirty films and heads her own production company.

Elijah and Ricci kiss in a scene from The Ice Storm. *Elijah was embarrassed to film this scene with his mother watching.*

The Ice Storm called for Elijah to explore a darker side of human nature. He plays Mike Carver, whose mother is having an affair with a married neighbor. His on-screen father meant so little to his character that when he arrives home from a business trip Elijah deadpans, "You were gone?" [26]

Uncomfortable Moments

The movie shows two sets of parents misbehaving and passing their tacit acceptance of immoral behavior on to their children. Without having their parents to act as a moral compass, the children in the movie are confused as they try to deal with their own emerging feelings toward the opposite sex. Creating these scenes was not always comfortable for the young actors. While making the movie, Elijah was thoroughly embarrassed by a kissing scene in an empty swimming pool with costar Christina Ricci. To his chagrin, it was filmed with his mother standing nearby. He was relieved she was not around when he filmed an intimate and odd scene with Ricci, in which she wore a mask of President Richard Nixon.

In real life, despite his protests of being too caught up in his career to have a girlfriend, Elijah was gingerly entering into a relationship with a girl. They had little time together, because of his busy schedule and the demands of her high school class schedule, but she would sometimes stop by his house before school. They would cuddle on the couch for a few moments before she had to leave for class. As is the case with many teen relationships, their time together as a couple was brief. Elijah was not ready to give a great deal of his time or emotional energy to a relationship. "The breakup was more about her needing me, and I didn't want to be with someone that needed me,"[27] he said.

Oliver Twist

Elijah preferred to focus on his career than worry about personal relationships. He enjoyed the experience of making a movie with emotional substance such as *The Ice Storm*. However, roles like that were few and far between for teen actors. For his next film, Elijah returned to the classics. He traveled to Ireland to play the Artful Dodger in a Disney adaptation of *Oliver Twist*, made for the television show *Wonderful World of Disney* and shown in November 1997.

In the role of a pickpocket who teaches Oliver how to steal, Elijah is called upon to be sneaky yet charming. However, with his bright blue eyes and clean good looks, it was difficult for him to pull off the Dodger's deceitful side. Elijah played an upbeat Dodger, and he seemed to enjoy the role and chance to act with film veteran Richard Dreyfus, who played Fagin, the rough, wily leader of a gang of boy thieves. The movie was entertaining and gave Elijah the opportunity to play a character with a dishonest side to him, but he did not look enough like a grimy street urchin in his attempt to portray a dishonest member of Fagin's gang. It would not be the last time his wholesome looks played against him.

Role Reversal

Elijah was carefully making the difficult transition into older teen roles, continuing to find work while appearing in films that did not compromise his moral values. Although his character and others in *The Ice Storm* did not always make the right choices, they all paid the price for their poor judgement. For his next picture, Elijah found a film that put a somewhat intelligent spin on his favorite genre, horror movies.

Elijah plays the Artful Dodger in the 1997 version of Oliver Twist. *Critics contended that his appearance was far too wholsome to play the roleof a desperate street urchin.*

Up to this point Elijah had appeared almost exclusively in serious adult movies and remakes of classics aimed at children and young adults. Now he decided to do something for himself, figuring there would be no harm in appearing in a fun movie that would not necessarily move his career forward. Elijah had been a horror movie fan for years, but he had been reluctant to use his talent for something so obviously cheesy. Then he read the script for *The Faculty.* It had elements of science fiction, teen angst, horror, and gore, a combination Elijah found to be an acceptable mix for his foray into teen horror films.

In *The Faculty,* Elijah plays Casey, a nerd among a group of students who must save the world from their teachers, who are really aliens. Although it is a horror movie, *The Faculty* is not a slasher film that relies only on gruesome scenes to bring chills to the audience. Elijah compared it to teen movies of the 1980s that he enjoyed, fantasies that were fun to watch.

Although Elijah did the movie as a fun rather than serious project, he approached his role with the same professionalism he put into his other work. His attitude impressed the movie's director, Richard Rodriguez. "Elijah Wood is the coolest kid I've ever met," Rodriguez said. "He has been in the business longer than most [kids] and he's still enthusiastic and confident. He's very charming, generous and genuine." [28]

The movie featured a cast of teen actors such as Jordana Brewster, Josh Hartnett of *Halloween: H2O,* and the singer Usher. They bonded over the chilling scenes they were filming, and Elijah enjoyed hanging out with the cast members. "It was basically like going away to summer camp," he said, adding, "except you're doing scenes where you have to freak out and run from scary objects and there's blood and stuff." [29]

There were rumors that he was dating Brewster, who also had a role in the soap opera *As the World Turns.* They went out to a New York club for a party given by clothing designer Tommy Hilfiger, but the relationship was not serious. Elijah said they only appeared together because both were doing ads for the designer's jeans.

Acting Tough

After *The Faculty,* Elijah turned down roles that cast him as a high school student. He did not have any actual high school ex-

Elijah appears in a scene from The Faculty, *a science fiction film about alien mind control.*

perience to draw on, and he wanted to stretch his acting ability beyond typical teen movies. His desire was to explore a variety of emotions and social situations through different characters.

A small role in the movie *Deep Impact* was his next project. The thriller looks at how people react after learning that a comet is hurtling toward earth. Elijah plays a boy who discovers that the comet is on its way and then must decide how to save his girlfriend from the probable destruction of the earth. In parallel story lines, Tea Leoni plays a reporter trying to connect with her father, and Morgan Freeman is the president who tries to hold

Elijah plays an inner-city hoodlum in Black and White. *This departure from his typical roles as a nice guy did little to advance his career.*

the country together. The movie did not deliver quite the emotional punch it was designed to, but it was not a flop. Elijah showed maturity by comfortably playing the role of a boyfriend as well as by venturing into new territory with an appearance in an action movie.

In his next movie, eighteen-year-old Elijah chipped away at his nice guy image. He took a big departure from his typical naïve, nice boy-next-door role in the 1999 movie *Black and White*. He had a small role in a movie with a large, eclectic cast of characters, playing a hip-hop wanna-be hanging out with a group of young adults.

With this part, he completely threw away his desire to play an upstanding character who would make a good role model. His character and the other teens in the movie have many undesirable habits, among them smoking, drugs, and promiscuity. His role as Wren was a world away from the surly but good-hearted and clean-cut Sandy he played in *Flipper*. In order to keep working through his teen years, though, Elijah had to prove himself by taking parts that played against his wholesome image. Throughout his life he had been infused with an energy that drove him to continue to look for work. Now in order to satisfy his desire to challenge himself as an actor, he had to back away from his resolve to take only parts that made him a role model.

His role in the movie was small, as he had to share screen time with a cast that included champion boxer Mike Tyson, model Claudia Schiffer, former child star Brooke Shields, and actor Robert Downey Jr. He and Brooke share a steamy kiss in the movie, filmed in New York's Central Park, and although he appeared to be less self-conscious about the kissing scene than he had in previous movies, his appearance in the movie did little to further his reputation as an actor. Elijah attempted to look tougher by dressing in street clothes. However, he still flashed his wide-eyed smile occasionally, and although he played the part of a jealous boyfriend he was still polite. The movie, which looks at teens struggling with identity and racial barriers, attracted some attention because of its large cast but failed to do well at the box office.

Bumbling Bumblebee

Elijah had yet to find a role that would define him as an actor who could successfully handle a meaty adult role. He tried another new tack with his next movie, *The Bumblebee Flies Anyway,* in which he plays an older teen searching for his identity. It was a mature leading role for Elijah and a chance for him to show his ability in a teen drama. The movie has science fiction overtones, with Elijah playing a teen who has had his memory erased. He is otherwise healthy, but as part of a memory experiment he must live at a facility for terminally ill children.

Elijah acted with younger children in the picture, which made the five-foot-six actor appear older and taller than he did in other films. He showcased his acting skill when displaying emotional pain, but the movie suffered from a predictable story line, slow pace, and unsatisfying ending. Elijah took a chance in the movie, trying to further his career with a dramatic lead as a wise teen. However, the role did not call for him to stretch his talent much beyond a narrow range of serious expressions. Elijah still had acting talent, but could not seem to find a way to put his years of experience to use in a movie that was worthy of his ability.

Doing the Right Thing

Elijah had been able to fulfill his goal of staying busy and continuing to make movies, but the films he was appearing in were not setting any box office records. The movies challenged him to try different types of roles but received a lukewarm reception from critics and moviegoers. However, Elijah was not one to feel sorry for himself. He was aware that sixteen was the top age for many child actors, and at age eighteen was thankful to continue working.

Elijah knew that to continue to act, he would need to stay firmly grounded and not get caught up in a self-indulgent Hollywood lifestyle. He did not react to a dip in his career with a rebellious interlude with drugs or alcohol. Elijah was not into the wild side of Hollywood. There were occasional appearances at movie premieres and trips out on the town with other cast members when

Unusual Audition

As *Lord of the Rings* director Peter Jackson began searching for an actor to play the role of Frodo, Elijah Wood was not a name that came to his mind. While Ian McKellen, who plays Gandalf, and Ian Holm, who plays Bilbo, had long been part of Jackson's wish list for the movie cast, he planned to have a British actor in the role of Frodo. He did not even know who Elijah was as he watched and turned down hundreds of hopefuls who auditioned for the part.

Elijah, however, was aware that Jackson was doing casting for *The Lord of the Rings,* and he was familiar with the director's previous work. He was a fan of Jackson's horror movies *Heavenly Creatures* (1994) and *The Frighteners* (1996), and he was intrigued by the prospect of working with the director and appearing in such an ambitious series of movies. He planned to show Jackson that he could be Frodo.

However, the auditions for the role of Frodo were held in London at the same time Wood was busy making the horror movie *The Faculty*. He could not leave the set to go to an audition halfway around the world. So, since he could not be there in person, Elijah did the next best thing.

Dressed in a rented costume, Elijah went to a wooded area, climbed a tree, and had a director friend film him as he read Frodo's lines from a book. His agent sent the tape to Jackson. When Elijah's audition tape showed up in the mail, Jackson did not recognize his name, but his writing partner, Fran Walsh, did. She was aware of his talent and interesting looks and encouraged Jackson to take a look at the tape. When Jackson viewed Elijah's audition tape, he knew he needed look no further for Frodo.

he was making a film, but for the most part he did not hang out with other actors and preferred to stay home. A self-described geek, he would rather get together with a group of friends and play Dungeons and Dragons than head out.

Elijah loved life too much to get mixed up with drugs or alcohol. He had admired the work of actor River Phoenix, who died of a drug overdose, and Elijah thought his death was senseless. Buoyed by support from his family, Elijah was too sensible to get mixed up in anything that would harm him. "I attribute a lot of my ability to deal with my success to the way my mother raised me," he said. "She gave me a strong base from which to realize who I am." [30]

Elijah thought about challenging himself by going to college, perhaps moving to Manhattan and studying English at Columbia

Elijah appears in a scene from The Faculty. *During the filming of* The Faculty, *Wood submitted an audition tape to director Peter Jackson for a part in* The Lord of the Rings.

University. He never got to see what college was like, however. While making *The Faculty,* Elijah had taped an audition for *The Lord of the Rings.* Director Peter Jackson had planned to cast a British actor in the role and screened more than two hundred unknowns, but when he saw Elijah's tape he was so impressed that he offered Elijah the major role of Frodo. "As soon as I saw the tape I knew we had found Frodo," Jackson said. "So Elijah cast himself in the film, really. We didn't have much to do with it." [31]

Elijah was about to embark on the most ambitious move of his career. He would have a central role in a big-budget production that would allow him to use the acting talent he had been shaping for most of his life. He had been experimenting with different roles and searching for ways to expand his acting repertoire, but now he would have the opportunity for a life experience of a depth he had never had before.

Chapter 5

The Ring's the Thing

IF THE SET of *The Faculty* was like summer camp for Wood, making the *Lord of the Rings* trilogy would be like going away to college. He was living away from home for the first time in his life, and during the fifteen months he spent shooting the three movies in New Zealand he established his independence and did a great deal of growing up. The work was arduous and exhausting, more than a year of long days and challenging scenes, but Wood embraced it all. He ultimately found that the only thing more difficult than making the movie was leaving the experience behind.

Weighty Role

Wood had the central role of Frodo in the *Lord of the Rings* trilogy. He was aware of the pressure that accompanied the weighty role in the much-anticipated movie. J.R.R. Tolkien had written the *Lord of the Rings* series sixty years before the movie was made, and the character of Frodo had been discussed and analyzed in English literature classes for decades. Wood was not certain his acting would measure up to the expectations people had for the character. "Every time you read a book it's your own journey, and millions of people have read these books, so I had that pressure on me," [32] he noted. Wood knew his interpretation of Frodo would be crucial to the success of the movies, and he accepted that responsibility. Rather than feeling daunted, he put his experience to work.

Wood saw parallels between his life and Frodo's journey, which helped him call up the necessary emotions for his part. Both were young men leaving home. Wood was eighteen when he left home to make the movies, and Frodo was just coming of age as a hobbit when he began the journey to destroy the ring. Both had an innocent quality about them, but were intrigued by what the world had to offer. The character Frodo was called upon to take the ring to its destruction and knew that others were depending on him to come through. Similarly, Wood was aware

Elijah Wood poses for a publicity photo in 2001, shortly before the release of The Fellowship of the Ring. *Elijah was initially daunted at the prospect of portraying Frodo in the* Lord of the Rings *trilogy.*

Making *The Lord of the Rings*

Director Peter Jackson had dreamed about making a movie version of the J.R.R. Tolkien trilogy *The Lord of the Rings* since he was eighteen. He was working as a photo engraver at a newspaper in Wellington when he read the books, and he thought they would make a fantastic film. It took twenty-two years for him to realize his dream, which could not have become a reality without the advanced special effects wizardry done by Weta Digital, part of Jackson's film company.

Flying beasts, a troll, warriors, and the elephant-like creatures that carried them were created in Weta Studios using a special software system. These creatures of Middle Earth came to life on the screen, but the actors who battled and interacted with them faced nothing but air while they were filming the movie. The digital creatures were added in the editing process and given life by a special effects team of artists, painters, animators, model makers, and others.

The creatures began as digital models. Then a digital skeleton and muscles were added to give them structure and movement. Texturing and lighting effects made characters such as Treebeard appear lifelike. The technology allowed Jackson and his crew to create a detailed and complex depiction of Middle Earth.

that his performance would play a large part in determining how the movies would be received, and that many people were depending on him to deliver a convincing portrayal of the movie's hero.

Grueling Schedule

Wood left California in the late summer of 1999 to begin making the movies in director Jackson's home country of New Zealand. He was awed by the beauty of the lush countryside and by the sunrises that spread rich colors over distant mountains. His appreciation for his picturesque surroundings helped temper the long days that he put in on the set. Wood rose at 4:30 or 5:00 A.M. to get into makeup. He stood for an hour and a half as his prosthetic hobbit feet were applied and then sat for another hour to get his wig, hobbit ears, and the rest of his makeup applied. After his makeup was done, he relaxed for a few minutes in the trailer he shared with the other actors who played hobbits and Sir Ian McKellen, who played the wizard Gandalf. He listened to music while getting ready to shoot his scenes for the day.

Always the professional, he kept a good attitude throughout the long shoot. His fellow actors were impressed by how quickly he could get into character, even though he was often tired from the rigorous filming schedule. The schedule was especially exhausting for Wood, who was in more scenes than the other characters. Filming often lasted until 8:00 P.M., and then Wood had to spend more than an hour and a half having his false feet and ears removed. He often wound down with friends at the end of the day, which cut into his sleep even more. To compensate, he took power naps during the day. He learned to fall asleep anywhere at any time and to awaken quickly and be ready to do a scene. He

Sir Ian McKelln and Elijah Wood share a smile at the 2001 premier of The Fellowship of the Ring. *Wood shared a trailer with the veteran British actor during the filming of the trilogy.*

developed a resilience that allowed him to bounce back. When he got tired, he remembered why he was there. Just recalling that he had been chosen to be part of the epic *Lord of the Rings* project lifted him up.

Showing Frodo's Dark Side

The *Lord of the Rings* series is comprised of three books, and Jackson felt the story could not be completely told in less than three movies. *The Fellowship of the Ring, The Two Towers,* and *The Return of the King* were to be filmed during the same shoot, which would take more than a year. Making things complicated for Wood and the other actors was the fact that the scenes were not shot in order. Wood could be making a scene for the first movie one day, and a scene for the third movie the next.

Wood's character grows progressively darker as the trilogy progresses, and he had to adjust his character's attitude depending on how far into the trilogy a scene went. The goodness that dominates Frodo's character at the beginning of the series is tainted by the power of the ring as the series progresses. Wood was intrigued by the way the character evolved through the series, and he enjoyed showing his character's transformation and growing obsession with power. "He starts out pure-hearted, but the ring chips away at the innocence and purity of Frodo's soul in the second (movie)," Wood said. "He starts to lose trust and faith in the people around him." [33]

The toughest part of the filming for Wood came from scenes later in the story, when he was called upon to act angry. This was an emotion that the upbeat Wood successfully supressed in real life—going so far as to replace harsh feelings for his father with calculated nonchalance. Because he kept his anger bottled up in his personal life, it was extremmly difficult for him to call it up on screen. Jackson needed Wood to show Frodo's emergent hatred, however, even if it was difficult. Jackson filmed several takes of a scene in which Frodo shows hate before Wood could convey the emotion in a way that pleased the director. Wood ultimately appreciated the opportunity to show his character's range of emotions and found his character's transformation to be the most interesting part of making the movie.

Finally, Friendship

The long days and difficult role could have made the fifteen months that Wood spent on the set of *The Lord of the Rings* the most difficult time of his life. But because he went through those experiences with wonderful cast members who became his friends, it was the best time he had ever had. Shortly after Wood arrived in New Zealand, his PlayStation2 burned out when he forgot to use a power transformer. He could not rely on playing video games to keep himself occupied between his takes. Instead of maintaining his insular interests, Wood had to let his guard down and make friends with his costars.

This was a new side of Wood, who learned to relax and laugh with his buddies. While his character in the movie starts to distrust his compatriots, Wood grew extremely close to his fellow actors in *Lord of the Rings*. The nine actors who played the members of the fellowship became compatriots as they depicted the adventures of the heros of Middle Earth.

In the *Rings* trilogy, the major characters band together to fight the armies created by the traitor wizard Saruman (played by Christopher Lee) and the dark and deeply evil Sauron, depicted in the first two movies as a flaming eye. While Wood's Frodo Baggins has the daunting task of taking the powerful One Ring to be destroyed in the fiery pits of Mordor, he gets support from a diverse group of compatriots. Closest to him are the hobbits Samwise Gamgee (Sean Astin), his loyal friend, and the happy-go-lucky Merry (Dominic Monaghan) and Pippin (Billy Boyd). The brave human ranger and future king Aragorn (Viggo Mortensen) is Frodo's valiant protector, while elf archer Legolas (Orlando Bloom), the determined dwarf Gimli (John Rhys-Davis), and the immortal wise wizard Gandalf (Ian McKellen) are his steadfast supporters. Also in the original fellowship is Boromir (Sean Bean), who has conflicting loyalties.

On-screen, the group comprising an elf, a dwarf, a wizard, hobbits, and humans were on a quest to save Middle Earth. Offscreen, the heroes were close friends who were immersed in the surreal experience of extended moviemaking. "I don't think I've ever been so close with people I've worked with in my life,"

True Friend

Sean Astin, who played Frodo's loyal friend, Sam, in *The Lord of the Rings*, was Elijah Wood's protector both on-screen and on the set of the movie. Astin, who was married and had two children, became sort of a role model for Wood. He took it upon himself to look after Wood, much as his character, Sam, looked after Wood's Frodo in the movie. "I sort of appointed myself as his minder," Astin said in an interview on the extended DVD edition of *The Lord of the Rings*. When Wood locked his keys in his apartment, it was Astin who arranged for a locksmith to come over and fix the situation.

Wood appreciated Astin's friendship. "He's a great guy, so genuine," Wood told Roger Moore of the Orlando Sentinel. Astin provided assistance to other cast members as well. After the movies were made, Dominic Monaghan needed a place to live in Los Angeles. Astin helped him find a place and also sold him his car. The son of actor John Astin and actress Patty Duke, Astin had a privileged Hollywood upbringing but did not insist on being pampered. Instead, he was driven by a desire to help others and make sure things were running smoothly.

Wood and other cast and crew members were able to repay Astin's kindness when he asked for some help with a project of his own. Astin was an aspiring filmmaker and wanted to make a short movie when the cast had a day off. Wood readily agreed to be in the *The Long and Short of It*. The short movie was filmed in a single day, and Wood became first assistant director of the project.

Wood and Sean Astin arrive at the 2001 premier of The Fellowship of the Ring. *Wood and Astin became close friends during the filming of the trilogy.*

Wood said. "I did a lot of growing up; I probably aged ten years . . . the person who went to New Zealand and the person who left there are significantly different." [34]

A Real Fellowship

The makeup that transformed Wood from human to hobbit was also worn by three other actors: Astin, Boyd, and Monaghan. Together the quartet endured the long, early morning ritual in the makeup trailer, made more enjoyable by the music from CDs that Wood provided. The makeup regimen was only one of the experiences that helped them form a common bond. Along with the other members of the fellowship, they learned to handle canoes, were helicoptered to remote locations to shoot scenes, and tried to stay comfortable in the sometimes freezing weather. "It was this amazing kind of coming together," Elijah said of the group. "It was this incredible excitement and anticipation for what we were about to do together." [35]

Although they had never met one another before they arrived in New Zealand, the group became extremely close during the time they spent together there. Jackson had hoped that this off-screen friendship would evolve to give their on-screen camaraderie an even deeper meaning. Because he had not met any of the other actors before filming began, Wood was unsure what to expect when he arrived in New Zealand. "I didn't know anyone and there's always that fear of going to someplace new and uncharted territory," [36] Wood said. He soon grew so close to his hobbit costars that they began referring to each other as hobbits offscreen as well. The actors played practical jokes on each other and other members of the cast. For example, after Bloom and Bean taped up Monaghan's trailer, Wood and Monaghan covered Bloom's trailer steps with fake dog poop.

Bloom, who played Legolas in *Rings,* taught Wood a few things about taking chances. The actors would wind down from hard work on the set with some intense play, and Bloom was always ready for an adventure. He encouraged Wood and the others to try a few of the extreme sports that lend themselves to New Zealand's landscape. Wood tried snowboarding and took up surfing, even buying his own surfboard. With his *Rings* costars, he showed the energetic side of his personality that had led his family to call him Sparkplug when he was a child. He felt comfortable enough with his circle of fellow actors to initiate ideas for fun, from acting as disc jockey for the cast and crew to offering a broad invitation after the day's shooting ended for people to join him at a Wellington night spot.

In some respects it was surprising that such a close friendship developed between the actors. The cast members who played the principal characters of the fellowship ranged in age from Wood, who was still a teenager, to Sir Ian McKellen, who was over sixty. Although their age differences spanned generations, it did not hinder the friendship that grew during the long months of shooting.

After filming ended, Wood commented that although he had compiled a long list of phone numbers of people whom he had acted with in the past, he never felt like he could call them and chat or ask for advice. Things were different with his *Rings* costars. "I don't think that will be true of someone like Ian McKellen," Wood said. "I look on him and the rest of the hobbit actors as true friends."[37] The British stage and screen veteran shared a trailer with Wood and the other hobbits during filming, and although he sometimes told them with mock anger that they needed to keep their music quieter, he praised their acting ability and enjoyed the experience of working with them.

The group had an easy rapport as they waited for shooting to begin or rehearsed a scene. With Boyd, Astin, and Monaghan, Wood relaxed, chatted, watched television, or visited movie theaters and some of the pubs in Wellington and other New Zealand communities. They ate meals together and wound down together after shooting was over for the day. Even though they worked together and hung around together, they did not tire of each other's company. Instead, their friendship grew stronger.

The nine actors who formed the fellowship grew so close that they decided to get a tattoo to commemorate their participation in the film. Wood, the other hobbits, Bloom, McKellen, Rhys-

Davies, and Mortensen and Bean, visited Wellington tattoo parlors to get the number nine, written in the Tolkien language of Elvish, tattooed in various places. Wood had his placed on his lower hip, an experience that was a painful one. As a sign of their friendship, McKellen held his hand while it was done. Wood described the experience: "It's like a hot, searing blade sawing into your skin." [38]

Difficult Farewell

The close rapport he established with his costars made the time Wood spent in New Zealand a wonderful period in his life. He had tasted independence and established frienships that were

Wood poses with his costars at the Sydney premier of The Fellowship of the Rings. *Wood formed a strong bond with each of his costars.*

closer than any he had ever experienced in his life. But while this made his time in New Zealand pass by quickly, it also made the months after he returned home extremely difficult.

Shooting for the majority of the movie ended a few days before Christmas in 2000. Wood and the other members of the cast had spent almost a year and a half away from home, immersed in a delightfully difficult project. The last month of shooting was intense, and the group had been working together for so long that it seemed the experience would never end. Then, abruptly, it did. The last day of shooting came and went, the cast and crew celebrated with a wrap party that night, and Wood and his costars flew home the next day. They knew they would be back for reshoots and finishing work on the project, but still felt an intense sense of sadness and loss now that their long journey through Middle Earth had come to an end.

Wood returned to his home in California exhausted from the tough shooting schedule but elated over what had been accomplished. Along the way he had tasted independence, camaraderie, and plain-old fun. Now he returned to a life that paled in comparison to the one he left behind.

As a reaction to the sudden change in lifestyle, Wood did something uncharacteristic. He did nothing. He did not want to go out on the town or even leave his house. He did not want to work. All he could bring himself to do was sit and listen to music or read a book. For the first time in his life, he sank into depression. "I have not wanted to stop before, but this gave me a powerful feeling of anti-climax," he said. "I had the world's best experience as an actor, and when it was all over I found it difficult to cope." [39]

For the next few years, Wood's life would be a series of ups and downs. At times he would be busy traveling, happily promoting the movie he had worked so hard on. There would also be trips to New Zealand for reshoots and voice dubbing. But there were also times when he wondered if this would be the best work he would ever do. "I think I am stronger as a result," he said two years after filming ended, "but for a while I did wonder whether I would ever find anything to match it. Here I am, still a young actor, thinking: 'Maybe this is as good as it gets.'" [40]

Ed Burns

Wood turned to Director Ed Burns for his first post-*Lord of the Rings* projects. Director, actor, and screenplay writer Ed Burns is known for turning out quality movies on a limited budget. His first movie, *The Brothers McMullen,* was made in 1995 for ten thousand dollars. It won the Grand Jury Prize at the Sundance Film Festival and brought Burns into the spotlight.

Burns grew up on Long Island in New York and studied film at Hunter College. He worked as a crew member of *Entertainment Tonight* and had numerous screenplays rejected by studios and agents before producing *The Brothers McMullen* himself. In 1996 he won the NATO/ShoWest award for Screenwriter of the Year.

Ed Burns poses for a photo in 2001. Burns is a talented screenwriter, director, and actor.

Wood knew the best way for him get over his feeling of loss would be to delve into a new project. He started reading scripts again and talked to director Ed Burns about his movie *Ash Wednesday*. Wood agreed to appear in the movie but later had second thoughts. He loved the idea of working with Burns on a low-budget project, the opposite of what he had just been through on the *Rings* set, but was not sure he had enough energy to give to the project. He almost backed out, but then thought better of it. He knew he needed to push himself to get beyond the comfort zone he had established on the set of *Rings*.

The lull Wood experienced after returning home from *The Lord of the Rings* would be short-lived. Soon he would have to jump on the promotional bandwagon for *The Fellowship of the Ring* and film a few more scenes for *The Two Towers*. He would also have to decide which direction to take his career and deal with an increased amount of interest from the public when his role as Frodo propelled his popularity to new heights.

Chapter 6

Attracting Attention

ALTHOUGH WOOD WAS a seasoned moviemaker, he had stayed below radar for much of his career. However, in the months before December 2001, when *The Lord of the Rings* was released, things got crazy. He received unprecedented attention for his role as the heroic Frodo and had to adjust to a new level of fame as well as the challenge of taking his career beyond the realm of Frodo and Middle Earth.

Wood was described as the ideal hobbit hero, and while this was a compliment to his acting ability it also meant that he drew more interest from fans and the media. Although he had been in the acting profession for years, he had never gone through anything like this before. Wood was noticed everywhere he went. Strangers came up to him and thanked him for his wonderful portrayal of Frodo. Once when he was at a juice bar with a reporter, a van with a photographer in it was nearby and the occupant was taking pictures of Wood. Wood quickly exited, not wanting to be the object of a tabloid story.

There were other examples that his fame was escalating. When he was having lunch at the Newsroom Café, comedian Chris Rock greeted him by loudly telling him he was a star. At the same restaurant, the meal was paid for by staff members because they enjoyed *The Fellowship of the Ring* so much. Wood also got his own action figure and, through his sister's acquaintance with Kelly Osbourne, a guest appearance on *The Osbournes* television show.

The flurry of attention surrounding *The Fellowship of the Ring* and its cast came as a surprise to Wood. He had expected it to be a major movie, but the twenty-year-old movie veteran was caught off guard by the amount of attention it drew from the press, public, and Academy Awards committee. *The Fellowship of the Ring* was nominated for thirteen Oscars, and by April 2002 had grossed more than $700 million worldwide.

Taking It in Stride

Although he was always upbeat when talking to the press or doing interviews, Wood was not awed or starstruck by his new level of popularity. He did not take credit for the success of the first *Rings* movie, although his character was the main focus of the story. Instead, he attributed the film's success to the way the movie was made. By immersing themselves in the world of Middle Earth for so long, he and the other actors had been able to make their performances especially compelling.

Wood was so nonchalant about the more dazzling side of stardom that he slept in on the morning the Academy Award nominations were announced and heard about the movie's nominations through messages on his answering machine. He almost dozed off at the 2002 Academy Awards ceremony, when he sat in the auditorium with his *Rings* costars. The movie won four Oscars, but the five-hour Academy Award show seemed boring to Wood, who would have preferred to watch it at home on television.

Returning to New Zealand in the spring of 2002 to shoot more scenes for *The Two Towers,* the second installment of the trilogy, was like a homecoming for Wood. He ate at his favorite breakfast spots and renewed his friendships with the cast and crew. Once again he experienced the satisfaction of working hard and enjoying every minute of it. He quickly renewed his friendships with other cast members, and they kept in touch after the additional scenes were shot. Wood visited and surfed with Boyd when Boyd was in Mexico making a movie with Russell Crowe. Wood and Boyd also celebrated the 2003 New Year together in the north of England, hitting the pubs with Monaghan in Boyd's hometown of Easterhouse. The trio also went pheasant hunting in the picturesque part of northern England known as the Lake District and took in a basketball game in New York shortly before the release of *The Two Towers.*

Family First

Wood had thoroughly enjoyed all the independence and freedom he had while living in New Zealand and making *The Lord of the Rings*. He also worked at maintaining the friendships he had forged while filming the movies. But when he was at home in California, his mother and siblings once again became the most important people in his life. Although he made millions in movies, he did not see himself placed above other members of his family. "I don't want to consider myself the breadwinner," he said. "It takes away the power and responsibility of my mother and the cohesive sense of family I have."[41]

Wood lived in a separate house on the family estate in Santa Monica, but he stopped by his mother's house each morning.

Wood signs autographs at the London premier of The Fellowship of the Ring. *The film made Wood a celebrity around the world.*

New Zealand

The stunning scenery that captivated Elijah Wood while he was making *The Lord of the Rings* captured the attention of movie audiences as well. After the movie was released, the number of tourists requesting information about the country doubled. The country's brilliant blue skies, majestic, snow-capped peaks, and jewel green valleys became sought-after destinations.

An island country in the Pacific Ocean, New Zealand is about one thousand miles southeast of Australia. It has two main islands and several dozen smaller ones. Its capital, Wellington, rests on a harbor on the North Island. Auckland, the largest city in New Zealand, is on the north end of the island and is built on volcanic hills. The country has a varied landscape, with mountains, waterfalls, sandy beaches, and fertile, green fields that provide pastures for sheep.

The movie trilogy proved to be a boon to the New Zealand travel industry because moviegoers wanted to see more of its breathtaking vistas. Tourists were assisted by the country's tourism website, www.purenz.com, and books such as *The Lord of the Rings, Locations Guide Book* by Ian Brodie, which told fans how to find the spots where some of the filming had been done.

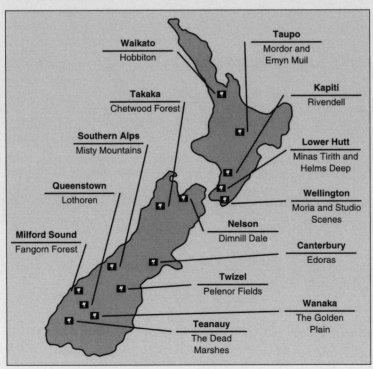

Waikato
Hobbiton

Taupo
Mordor and
Emyn Muil

Takaka
Chetwood Forest

Kapiti
Rivendell

Southern Alps
Misty Mountains

Lower Hutt
Minas Tirith and
Helms Deep

Queenstown
Lothoren

Wellington
Moria and Studio
Scenes

Nelson
Dimnill Dale

Milford Sound
Fangorn Forest

Canterbury
Edoras

Twizel
Pelenor Fields

Wanaka
The Golden
Plain

Teanauy
The Dead
Marshes

His mother still did his laundry and cooked his meals for him, and he did not apologize for not being more independent. "I wake up in the morning, go to Mom's house, have a cup of coffee and chat," he said. "She likes the same music that I do, so she'll have the White Stripes on. How cool is that?"[42] He knew he likely would not live at home forever, however, and when he reached age twenty-two he began making plans to have his own place.

Wood also remained close to his brother, a video game producer in San Diego, and sister, who dabbled in poetry. However, his relationship with his father remained cool, and he kept his feelings about his father buried under the business of his day-to-day life. One uncomfortable offshoot of his fame was the additional attention his relationship with his father received. When reporters asked about his father, he learned to reply in a detached manner. Although at times Wood's eyes got glassy when talking about his father, he maintained an unemotional tone of voice when discussing his father's distance from the family. He was especially upset that when his father called the family at Christmas, he had left a message saying that he wanted to talk to Elijah, or anyone else who was around. Wood was too close to his siblings and mother to want a relationship with his father that would relegate them to a lower level of attention.

Quiet Lifestyle

Wood was not interested in attracting undue attention to himself beyond what was required for him to continue to receive notable scripts to read and movie offers to consider. He had enjoyed going out with his friends from the *Rings* cast while filming in New Zealand, but back home he preferred to keep to himself rather than enjoy the Hollywood nightlife scene. He usually attended a movie premiere only when he was in the film and sometimes avoided the party after to avoid an uncomfortable social situation.

Wood was not friendless in Hollywood, however. He sometimes hung out with MTV personality Iann Robinson or other friends who shared his interest in music. Wood's demeanor impressed Robinson. Although Wood had talent and money, he did not have the arrogance that usually accompanied it. His favorite pastimes included playing video games or shopping for CDs at the Amoeba music store in Los Angeles. Wood did not relish being recognized by fans, but when he was noticed he was gracious about it, offering them a comment or compliment and showing the genuine side of his personality.

Playing Against His Character

Wood's pleasant personality and boyish looks made him popular with fans, but caused him some problems in his career. It was difficult for people to envision him as anything other than a nice character. He considered different roles as he looked to move beyond the part of Frodo. As wonderful as his performance had been, he did not want it be the last big part he ever had or the climax of his acting career. To this end, he tried to expand his acting repertoire and showcase his range of abilities.

In the spring of 2002, Wood made *Try Seventeen*. He wanted to avoid being typecast as a fantasy or period-film actor and return to films set in a more modern time frame. In the comedy, he plays a university student who drops out of school and learns about life from the characters who inhabit his apartment building. His costars in the movie include pop star Mandy Moore and Deborah Harry, former lead singer of the band Blondie.

Wood hoped for more success with that role than he had had in another attempt to play against his character. His role as a murderous member of a tough Irish mafia family in *Ash Wednesday* met with criticism. The movie was was released in spring 2002, a few months after Wood had received rave reviews for his role as Frodo, and his clean looks did not fit in with the film's scruffy characters. "Wood has been good in a few pictures, but his distinctly boyish looks and voice are far better suited to roles that place him in the lands of Middle-Earth than as a tough on the streets of Hell's Kitchen,"[43] wrote reviewer Scott Foundas. Wood had succeeded in landing a part that took him into new territory, but he was not able to bring it alive successfully.

Also released in 2002 was the animated video *The Adventures of Tom Thumb and Thumbelina*. Wood had done the voice work

Video Maniac

One of the bonuses of being part of *The Lord of the Rings* series for Elijah Wood was getting a chance to be a character in the video games the series spawned. As soon as he heard that a *Lord of the Rings* game was being discussed, his ears perked up. A huge game fan, he wanted to find out all he could. Wood admitted that he enjoyed playing video games so much that he got into stretches with adventure games where he played all the time. Once he got his head into the game, he could not pull himself away until his character reached the end.

On *The Lord of the Rings: The Two Towers* video game, he did voice work, adding the sound that enchanced the sword fights and also adding a few words of dialog. Although Frodo was not one of the characters players could control, Wood thought it was cool to see himself running around on a video game. "I'm a fan of action figures and I'm a fan of games so if I get to be included in it it's a total geek bonus. I dig it," he said in an interview featured on bonus material on *The Lord of the Rings: The Two Towers* video game.

for the video a few years before it was released. The video did little to either hurt or help his career. A bland but harmless story about the adventures of two tiny people, it also featured Jennifer Love Hewitt as the voice of Thumbelina.

Although not always successful, Wood's forays into post-*Rings* movies were something of a declaration of independence for him. He played much more of a dominant role in his career than he had when he was younger, when he relied on his mother to make the majority of his decisions for him. Now he was calling the shots, for better or for worse. A veteran of movies both good and bad, he had learned long ago to let go of the movie once he was done with his role and not worry too much about the finished product.

The Two Towers

Wood's fame received a boost each holiday season as the *Rings* movies were released, although Wood's character of Frodo did not have as central a role in the final two installments of the trilogy. While he was still crucial to the story line and had some heroic soul-searching to do, his story had been the main focus of the initial installment. The second, *The Two Towers,* concentrated more

Wood leaves a press conference for The Two Towers. *Despite his success as Frodo, Wood took on veying roles to avoid being typecast as a fantasy actor.*

on the wizard Gandalf's battle with evil, and the third, *The Return of the King,* to be released in December 2003, would place more emphasis on Aragorn.

Wood still did his share of interviews when the second installment was released in December 2002. Earlier in the year he had been the subject of a story in *Rolling Stone,* and now that the release of the second movie was drawing closer he did numerous interviews with newspaper reporters and radio hosts. He was interviewed for a cover story for *YM* and appeared on talk shows with Jay Leno and Regis and Kelly, as well as making an appearance on the *Today* show. He sported a new, close-cropped haircut that generated a good deal of conversation, and he was upbeat as he talked about the experience he had while making *The Two Towers.*

Wood explained how he enjoyed seeing Frodo take on a darker tone in this movie. As Frodo began to be tested by the temptation of the ring, Wood had the opportunity to add more depth to his character by showing both his good and evil sides. This was the part of his character that Wood had the most difficulty with, and some reviewers felt his inner conflict was not heavy or genuine enough to convince viewers that he was anything but a bright-eyed hero. However, others felt he accurately conveyed the power of the ring, which could both empower and seduce the one who held it.

A computer generated character named Gollum generated much attention from the press during the early days of the movie's release, but Wood's association with the movie was sealed. There was a question, however, of whether he would build on the success he had generated with the role or if the role would be the crowning achievement of his career.

Always Busy

As 2003 began, Elijah's mood began to change. He felt like making movies again. His work was not just a way for him to lift himself out of a post–New Zealand fog but was for his own enjoyment. After the filming of *Rings* ended, he had questioned his ability and wondered whether he would ever be able to match his performance as Frodo and live up to people's ever-growing expectations of him as an actor. He had come through that period of self doubt and was comfortable with his career and confident about his future. "My life is so calm and normal," he said. "Yes, the success of the films has changed my life but not in such a way that

I can't go on about my life as I have before. I've been working since I was eight and to have a career before LOTR and have that time of gradual growth has been a good learning experience in dealing with the added amount of attention."[44]

The success of the *Rings* movies opened up new opportunities for him. In 2003 he had a supporting role in *Eternal Sunshine of the Spotless Mind* with Jim Carrey and Kate Winslet. In the comedy, Carrey and Winslet play a couple who want to have bad memories of their relationship erased, and Wood plays a technician who helps them.

Wood wanted to get his career to the point where he would have his choice of directors and intriguing roles. He definitely wanted to keep acting, and he also considered dabbling in film editing. He continued to be challenged by his work and wanted to keep growing and improving. After working in the world of adults for most of his life, he finally felt like his numerical age had caught up with his emotional one, and he was ready to take on interesting adult roles.

The life he had lived as an actor would be both a help and hindrance as he strove to reach his goal. He had a wealth of acting experience to draw on and had turned in enough successful performances to get immediate consideration for a wide variety of projects. He had been part of an epic series of movies that were destined to become classics, and he would always be associated with their success. However, he would also have to be careful not

Intrigued by Gollum

Frodo spent part of the movie *The Two Towers* interacting with a character named Gollum, who had been played by Andy Serkis on the set. In the movie, a computer-generated character was superimposed over Serkis's body to give him a creepy, hunched appearance. His hissing voice and weird appeal became one of the most talked-about aspects of the movie.

The love-hate relationship Gollum had with himself and the ring made him both pitiable and disgusting, a combination moviegoers found freakish yet intriguing. Wood thought Gollum to be one of the most interesting characters in the movie. If he had to choose another character to play in the series, he would be Gollum.

Wood poses at the 2002 premier of The Two Towers. *Elijah Wood has appeared in over thirty films, and he plans to maintain his busy career.*

to let the success of the *Rings* movies overshadow his ability to play a variety of roles.

A childhood spent making movies could make it challenging for him to bring complex roles to life, as he has been sheltered from some of the uncomfortable yet important aspects of growing up. His life as a child actor may not have given him the wealth and depth of experiences he will need to create believable characters. He had never had to learn to work through the awkward and sometimes painful situations that come with the social encounters of children and teens. And the situation that is likely to cause him the most pain in his life—his relationship with his father—has been buried so deep that he has become numb to his feelings toward it. His inability to draw on these emotions will be a challenge to his career, as he will have to learn to convey emotions that he has not had practice mastering.

In his favor are his solid work ethic and dependable nature. He has not gotten sidetracked with the excesses of Hollywood that derail so many young actors. He does not obsess about his fame or let it interfere with his daily life. Even a reminder of his most precious role is kept hidden away. He has one of the rings that was used as a prop during the making of *The Lord of the Rings,* but he does not wear it. Instead, he prefers a ring he purchased with a Hebrew inscription that translates to "If it doesn't happen now, when will it?" He is ready for his next challenge and willing to go for the opportunities that come his way. Wood has compiled a long list of acting credits during a career that he has enjoyed since he was eight, but is not content to rest on what he has accomplished. Because he enjoys what he does, he will continue to look forward to more challenges and actively maintain his busy career.

Notes

Chapter 1: Opening Act

1. Quoted in Patty Adams, "The Mysterious Mr. Wood," *YM,* January 2003, p. 55.

Chapter 2: Acting for Adults

2. David Hiltbrand, "Child of the Night," *People Weekly,* April 30, 1990, p. 17.
3. Quoted in Lisa Degnan, *Elijah Wood: Hollywood's Hottest Rising Star.* New York: Warner, 1999, p. 36.
4. Quoted in Associated Press, "Huck Finn Finally Comes of Age–12," *Greensboro News Record,* June 4, 1993, p. D4.
5. Ty Burr, "Forever Young," *Entertainment Weekly,* June 11, 1993, p. 62.
6. Henry Sheehan, "Twain's Tale Is Tamed," *Orange County Register,* April 2, 1993, p. 16.
7. Quoted in Adams, "The Mysterious Mr. Wood," p. 55.
8. Quoted in Adams, "The Mysterious Mr. Wood," p. 55.

Chapter 3: Rising Star

9. Quoted in Associated Press, "Huck Finn Finally Comes of Age–12," p. D6.
10. Glenn Kenny, "The Good Son," *Entertainment Weekly,* December 16, 1994, p. 81.
11. Quoted in Ty Burr, "The Revelation of Elijah," *Entertainment Weekly,* November 25, 1994, p. 38.
12. Quoted in Associated Press, "Huck Finn Finally Comes of Age–12."

13. Quoted in Associated Press, "Huck Finn Finally Comes of Age–12," p. D6.
14. Quoted in Degnan, *Elijah Wood,* p. 55.
15. Quoted in Burr, "The Revelation of Elijah," p. 38.
16. Quoted in Burr, "The Revelation of Elijah," p. 38.
17. Quoted in Sulain Moy, "Well Twained at Twelve," *Entertainment Weekly,* April 2, 1993, p. 61.
18. Quoted in Kevin D. Thompson, "Role as Troubled Teen Concerns 'Flipper' Star," *Times Union,* May 20, 1996, p. C5.
19. Quoted in Mal Vincent, "Behind the Scenes with Elijah Wood, Paul Hogan and 'Flipper,'" Knight Ridder/Tribune, 1996.
20. Quoted in Vincent, "Behind the Scenes with Elijah Wood, Paul Hogan and 'Flipper.'"
21. Quoted in *Flipper,* directed by Alan Shapiro, distributed by Universal Studios Home Video, 1996, videocassette.
22. Quoted in "Talking to . . . Elijah Wood," *Teen,* June 1996, p. 68.

Chapter 4: Experimental Phase

23. Quoted in Chris Heath, "The Secret Life of Elijah Wood," *Rolling Stone,* April 11, 2002, p. 57.
24. Quoted in Heath, "The Secret Life of Elijah Wood."
25. Quoted in Alan Palmer, "Elijah on Life After 'Lord of the Rings.'" www.mirror.co.uk.
26. Quoted in *The Ice Storm,* directed by Ang Lee, distributed by 20th Century Fox Home Entertainment, 1997.
27. Quoted in Heath, "The Secret Life of Elijah Wood."
28. Quoted in Degnan, *Elijah Wood,* p. 66.
29. Quoted in Degnan, *Elijah Wood,* p. 27.
30. Quoted in William Russell, "Elijah's Teenage Kicks," *Herald* (Glasgow), April 8, 1999, p. 16.
31. Quoted in Steven Rea, "For Director, Making 'Lord of the Rings' Is the Ultimate Fantasy," Knight Ridder/Tribune, December 21, 2001.

Chapter 5: The Ring's the Thing

32. Quoted in Steve Zahn, "Elijah Wood: The Hobbit Who's About to Become a Hollywood Habit," *Interview,* December 2001, p. 103.

33. Quoted in Adams, "The Mysterious Mr. Wood," p. 55.
34. Quoted in Adams, "The Mysterious Mr. Wood," p. 55.
35. Quoted in *The Lord of the Rings: The Fellowship of the Ring*, directed by Peter Jackson, distributed by New Line Home Entertainment, 2002, special extended DVD edition.
36. Quoted in *The Lord of the Rings: The Fellowship of the Ring*, DVD.
37. Quoted in Palmer, "Elijah on Life After 'Lord of the Rings.'"
38. Quoted in Adams, "The Mysterious Mr. Wood," p. 55.
39. Quoted in Palmer, "Elijah on Life After 'Lord of the Rings.'"
40. Quoted in Palmer, "Elijah on Life After 'Lord of the Rings.'"

Chapter 6: Attracting Attention

41. Quoted in Heath, "The Secret Life of Elijah Wood," p. 57.
42. Quoted in Adams, "The Mysterious Mr. Wood," p. 55.
43. Scott Foundas, "Ash Wednesday," *Variety*, May 20, 2002, p. 26.
44. Quoted in Comingsoon.net, "Interviews: Elijah Wood Talks *The Two Towers!*" December 13, 2002. www.comingsoon.net.

Important Dates in the Life of Elijah Wood

1981

Elijah Wood is born on January 28 in Cedar Rapids, Iowa.

1989

An agent spots Elijah at a talent convention in Los Angeles and tells him and his mother that Elijah could have a future in acting; Elijah and his family move to Los Angeles, and he is soon cast in Paula Abdul's video "Forever Your Girl"; a small part in *Back to the Future II* is Elijah's first appearance on the big screen.

1990

Elijah has a small role in *Internal Affairs* and a major one in *Avalon*.

1992

A dramatic role in *Radio Flyer* and a part opposite Mel Gibson in *Forever Young* solidify Elijah's reputation as a young actor.

1993

Elijah takes on the classic role of Huckleberry Finn in a Disney movie and plays a good kid opposite Macaulay Culkin's evil character in *The Good Son*.

1994

Solid performances in *North* and *The War* earn Elijah the ShoWest Award for Young Star of the Year, as well as a Saturn Award.

1996

The dolphins are the best part of Elijah's experience on the set of *Flipper*.

1997

Elijah establishes himself as an actor who is ready for older roles in *The Ice Storm* and takes on another classic with a performance as the Artful Dodger in *Oliver Twist.*

1998

With *The Faculty,* Elijah realizes a dream of appearing in a horror film; he appears in *Deep Impact,* a thriller with heart; while on the set of *The Faculty,* he hears that auditions are being done for *The Lord of the Rings* and mails a taped audition to director Peter Jackson.

1999

The movie *Black and White* does not do much for Elijah's career, but he lands the defining role of Frodo in *The Lord of the Rings* anyway; late in the year he travels to New Zealand and spends fifteen months making the three movies in series.

2000

The Bumblebee Flies Anyway and *Chain of Fools,* which were made before Elijah left for New Zealand, are released.

2001

Elijah's career reaches new heights after *The Lord of the Rings: The Fellowship of the Ring* is released to widespread acclaim.

2002

Elijah follows up his appearance in the big-budget *Lord of the Rings* with an appearance in the independent film *Ash Wednesday; The Lord of the Rings: The Two Towers* is released, and Elijah again earns praise for his role as Frodo; also released is the animated movie *The Adventures of Tom Thumb and Thumbelina,* with Elijah as the voice of Tom Thumb.

2003

Eager to expand his acting repertoire, Elijah appears in *Try Seventeen* and makes *Eternal Sunshine of the Spotless Mind;* the final installment of *The Lord of the Rings* trilogy, *The Return of the King,* is released.

For Further Reading

Books

Lisa Degnen, *Elijah Wood: Hollywood's Hottest Rising Star.* New York: Warner, 1999. A photo-heavy look at Elijah's career before he made *The Lord of the Rings*.

Brian Sibley, *The Lord of the Rings: The Making of the Movie Trilogy.* Boston: Houghton Mifflin, 2002. A look at how the cast and crew worked to create an authentic tale of Middle Earth.

———, *The Lord of the Rings: The Official Movie Guide.* Boston: Houghton Mifflin, 2001. The thoughts of Elijah, director Peter Jackson, and others on J.R.R. Tolkien's work and what it meant to bring it to the screen.

Periodicals

Patty Adams, "The Mysterious Mr. Wood," *YM,* January 2003.

"Talking to . . . Elijah Wood," *Teen,* June 1996.

Websites

TheOneRing.net (www.theonering.net). This website has everything there is to know about *The Lord of the Rings* and what the cast of the movie trilogy is up to.

Always and Forever: Elijah Wood (www.always.ejwsites.net). This website has an extensive collection of Elijah Wood news, interviews, and articles.

Internet Movie Database (www.imdb.com). This website offers a biography, pictures of Elijah, and a list of his films, as well as discussions about them.

Works Consulted

Periodicals

David Ansen, "A 'Ring' to Rule the Screen," *Newsweek,* December 10, 2001.

Associated Press, "Huck Finn Finally Comes of Age—12," *Greensboro News Record,* June 4, 1993.

Hannah Brown, "US Director Here for Eilat Festival," *Jerusalem Post,* March 24, 2003.

Ty Burr, "Forever Young," *Entertainment Weekly,* June 11, 1993.

———, "The Revelation of Elijah," *Entertainment Weekly,* November 25, 1994.

Richard Corliss, "The Ice Storm," *Time,* September 29, 1997.

Gillian Flynn, "The Power of Towers," *Entertainment Weekly,* November 15, 2002.

Scott Foundas, "Ash Wednesday," *Variety,* May 20, 2002.

Owen Gleiberman, "Tolkien Effort," *Entertainment Weekly,* December 13, 2002.

Chris Heath, "The Secret Life of Elijah Wood" *Rolling Stone,* April 11, 2002.

David Hiltbrand, "Child of the Night," *People Weekly,* April 30, 1990.

———, "Dayo," *People Weekly,* May 4, 1992.

Joanne Kaufman, "North," *People Weekly,* August 8, 1994.

Geoff Keighley, "It's in the Baggins," *Entertainment Weekly,* October 25, 2002.

Terry Kelleher, "Oliver Twist," *People Weekly,* November 17, 1997.

Glenn Kenny, "The Good Son," *Entertainment Weekly,* December 16, 1994.

Stuart Klawans, "Avalon," *Nation,* November 5, 1990.

Roger Moore, "Rings Star Has Made Niceness a Hobbit," *Los Angeles Times,* January 20, 2003.

Sulain Moy, "Well Twained at Twelve," *Entertainment Weekly,* April 2, 1993.

Lisa Nellelson, "The Bumblebee Flies Anyway," *Variety,* September 27, 1999.

Ralph Novak, "The War," *People Weekly,* November 14, 1994.

Troy Patterson, "Elvish Lives!" *Entertainment Weekly,* August 9, 2002.

Jill Rachlin, "The Adventures of Huck Finn," *Entertainment Weekly,* April 12, 1993.

Robin Rauzi, "Career Not Kid's Stuff for This Kid," *Cleveland Plain Dealer,* April 30, 1993.

Steven Rea, "For Director, Making 'Lord of the Rings' Is the Ultimate Fantasy," Knight Ridder/Tribune, December 21, 2001.

William Russell, "Elijah's Teenage Kicks," *Herald* (Glasgow), April 8, 1999.

Lisa Schwarzbaum, "Force of Hobbit," *Entertainment Weekly,* December 14, 2001.

Henry Sheehan, "Twain's Tale Is Tamed," *Orange County Register,* April 2, 1993.

"Talking to . . . Elijah Wood," *Teen,* June 1996.

Kevin D. Thompson, "Role as Troubled Teen Concerns 'Flipper' Star," *Times Union,* May 20, 1996.

Ken Tucker, "Flipper," *Entertainment Weekly,* May 24, 1996.

Mal Vincent, "Behind the Scenes with Elijah Wood, Paul Hogan and 'Flipper,'" Knight Ridder/Tribune, 1996.

Charles Winecoff, "The Adventures of Huck Finn," *Entertainment Weekly,* December 3, 1993.

Steve Zahn, "Elijah Wood: The Hobbit Who's About to Become a Hollywood Habit," *Interview,* December 2001.

Internet Sources

Comingsoon.net, "Elijah Wood Talks *The Two Towers*," December 13, 2002, www.comingsoon.net.

Ryan J. Downey, "Elijah Wood Plays DJ for *Try Seventeen* co-star Mandy Moore," www.mtv.com.

Alan Palmer. "Elijah on Life After 'Lord of the Rings.'" www.mirror.co.uk.

Movies

Flipper, directed by Alan Shapiro, distributed by Universal Studios Home Video, 1996, videocassette.

The Ice Storm, directed by Ang Lee, distributed by 20th Century Fox Home Entertainment, 1997, DVD.

The Lord of the Rings: The Fellowship of the Ring, directed by Peter Jackson, distributed by New Line Home Entertainment, 2002, special extended DVD edition.

Video Games

The Lord of the Rings: The Two Towers, distributed by Electronic Arts, 2002.

Index

105

Picture Credits

About the Author

Terri Dougherty is a freelance writer from Appleton, Wisconsin. In addition to nonfiction books for children, she also writes magazine and newspaper articles. A native of Black Creek, Wisconsin, Terri graduated from the University of Wisconsin-Oshkosh. She was a reporter and editor at the *Oshkosh Northwestern* daily newspaper for five years before beginning her freelance writing career. In her spare time, Terri plays soccer and reads. She enjoys cross-country skiing and attending plays with her husband, Denis, and swimming, biking, and playing with their three children—Kyle, Rachel, and Emily.